MA AND PA
DRACULA

Other books by
ANN M. MARTIN:

Yours Turly, Shirley

Ten Kids, No Pets

Slam Book

Just a Summer Romance

Missing Since Monday

With You and Without You

Me and Katie (the Pest)

Stage Fright

Inside Out

Bummer Summer

BABY-SITTERS LITTLE SISTER series
THE BABY-SITTERS CLUB series

ANN M. MARTIN

MA AND PA DRACULA

Interior drawings by Dirk Zimmer

AN
APPLE
PAPERBACK

SCHOLASTIC INC.
New York Toronto London Auckland Sydney

This book is for
WENDY KERBY,
VERONICA JACKSON,
and
JOLYNN CRUTCHER

ISBN 0-590-43828-X

Text copyright © 1989 by Ann M. Martin. Illustrations copyright © 1989 by Dirk Zimmer. All rights reserved. This edition published by Scholastic Inc., 730 Broadway, New York, NY 10003, by arrangement with Holiday House, Inc. APPLE PAPERBACKS is a registered trademark of Scholastic Inc.

12 11 10 9 8 7 6 5 4 3 2   1 2 3 4 5 6/9

Printed in the U.S.A.   40

First Scholastic printing, November 1991

Contents

MA AND PA DRACULA

1

Moving

The rattly old car sped through the night. Jonathan Primave stared into darkness.

"Go to sleep, Jonathan," said Mr. Saginaw, Jonathan's tutor.

But Jonathan couldn't. No one else was asleep. Besides, he only got to ride in a car once or twice a year—whenever his family moved. Jonathan didn't want to miss a thing.

In the front seat, Mrs. Primave began to scream. "Vlad! Look out! Look out, Vlad! Look out, look out, look out!"

Mr. Primave hit the brakes.

EEEEEEEECH! The car skidded to a stop.

Mr. Primave turned to his wife. "What was it? What did you see?"

"I saw, um . . . I—I saw . . ."

"Dear, if you are going to screech every ten minutes, then perhaps *you* should drive," said Jonathan's father.

"No, no, no. That is quite all right. I have not driven in decades," replied Mrs. Primave. "I do not wish to start in the dark, while we are pulling the trailer. I will just help you."

Mr. Primave sighed. "Do not help me too much, though," he said.

Jonathan looked at his parents. He could barely see them. The car was stopped on an out-of-the-way country road. There were no streetlights or houselights—only the light from a round, full moon.

Although Ma and Pa were husband and wife—not related at all, of course—they looked remarkably alike. Both had black hair, although Pa's was short, and Ma's was so long she could coil it around and around on her head. Their teeth were white and straight, with two long pointy ones on the top, on either side. Their fingernails looked like claws and their ears were pointed. An interesting thing that Jonathan had noticed was that he and Mr. Saginaw did not have fangs or claws. Jonathan just supposed that parents did, and boys and tutors did not. Ma and Pa were very, very thin and their skin was icy-cold. (Jonathan and Mr. Saginaw were nicely rounded with pleasant, warm skin.)

Another interesting thing that Jonathan noticed was that in the evening, when his parents woke up, their dark eyes were lifeless—no sparkle—and their skin was deathly white. But by morning, when they returned from work and were ready to go to bed, their eyes were bright and their skin flushed red.

Oh, well, thought Jonathan. Some people never looked good first thing in the evening.

Sometimes Jonathan wondered how old Ma and Pa were.

He had asked them a number of times but had never gotten a straight answer. Once Ma had said, "As old as the hills." Once Pa had said, "Old enough." Once Ma had said, "Older than you." And once Pa had said, "Two hundred and twelve."

Jonathan jumped as Pa started the car with a jerk. It shook and rattled and coughed and sputtered. Jonathan thought that was how all cars sounded when they started up. That was because he had never known any other cars.

Once he'd read about a fancy, smooth-sounding car in a book, but that hardly counted. An author could write anything in a book. Jonathan's parents had lectured him about that lots of times. How often had Ma or Pa said to him, "Do not believe everything you read, Jonathan"?

They said it every time Jonathan asked a question like, "Ma, why is it that in all these books, the people are awake during the *day*—when it's light outside—and asleep during the *night*—when it's dark outside? That is how these people live, Ma. Are some people really like that?"

And Mrs. Primave had said, "Do not believe everything you read, Jonathan."

That had also been the Primaves's answer when Jonathan had said, "The boy in this book goes to a place called *school*," and when he'd said, "The girl in this book keeps a dog in her house," and again when he'd said, "These children leave their house and play outside."

But the night Jonathan said, "I read about a boy who watches something called TV," Ma and Pa sprang into action.

"Where did you get that book?" asked Ma. "You know TV is make-believe, do you not?"

"How much do you know about TV?" asked Pa. "Did it mention radio?"

Ma had elbowed Pa in the ribs then, and the Primaves had called in Mr. Saginaw.

"Jonathan read about *TV*," they'd said accusingly.

Poor Mr. Saginaw, Jonathan thought as the car screeched along. He had felt sorry for him. "I did not *mean* to read about it," Jonathan had apologized, "but it was right there. It was in that book about the chocolate factory."

"Ah . . . harrumph." Mr. Saginaw had adjusted his wire-rimmed glasses. Nervously, he'd straightened his necktie and slicked his hair back. "That would have been *Charlie and the Chocolate Factory* by Mr. Roald Dahl," he had said, and harrumphed again.

Mr. Saginaw was the primmest, most proper person Jonathan knew. (Although he was the *only* person Jonathan knew, apart from Ma and Pa.) Mr. Saginaw cared deeply for Jonathan, but he had difficulty showing his feelings. Mostly he just harrumphed. He harrumphed when he was nervous or upset or pleased.

Mr. Saginaw had helped to raise Jonathan. He cooked all their meals and ate them alone with Jonathan. Ma and Pa never ate. Not at home, anyway. Jonathan supposed they ate at work. They left for work each evening, soon after Jonathan had woken up. At dawn, they returned, not long before it was time to go to bed. While they were away, Mr. Saginaw tutored Jonathan. This is what happened seven days a week, year round. It was the only life Jonathan had known.

Jonathan leaned back as the car whizzed through the night. He glanced at Mr. Saginaw, who was sitting next to him, falling asleep. Mr. Saginaw had taught Jonathan how to read. He was in charge of picking out his books. That was why, when Ma and Pa found out about the chocolate-factory book, they had been upset with Mr. Saginaw.

"Why did you select that book for Jonathan?" Mr. Primave had asked.

"Well, it seemed so utterly silly," said Mr. Saginaw. "It is the story of a youngster, Charlie Bucket, who wins a trip through a chocolate factory. I have made it clear to Jonathan that fiction is entirely made up. Nothing about it is true at all."

That was how Jonathan knew that authors could write whatever they felt like writing. It was also how he knew that there were no such things as school or TV or VCRs or friends or people who sleep at nighttime. Those things were as fictitious as witches and ghosts and vampires.

Weren't they?

Actually, Jonathan didn't give it much thought. He knew what he knew. And what he knew was his life:

Every evening, Jonathan woke up when his alarm clock rang. (Pa always set Jonathan's alarm before the Primaves went to bed in the morning.) The clock would go off just as darkness was falling. Jonathan had never seen bright sunlight. He had never been outside of his house—except to move.

From what Jonathan could tell in the little he saw from his bedroom window each evening, he and Mr. Saginaw and his parents always lived far out in the country, usually in an old, isolated farmhouse.

And wherever they lived, their routine was the same. After Jonathan's alarm clock rang, he would get dressed and go downstairs for breakfast. On the way, he would pass Ma and Pa's bedroom. Their door would be open, the bed neatly made. No matter how fast Jonathan got dressed, his parents always beat him downstairs. And they always said that they were not going to eat breakfast, or that they were going to go out for breakfast. So Jonathan and Mr. Saginaw would eat together. Then Mr. Saginaw would tutor Jonathan.

Jonathan's life had been like this for nine years and three months. If it seemed odd, he didn't bother to wonder about it for long. It was just his life.

Then one evening—the evening before the car trip—Jonathan ran downstairs and found Ma and Pa and Mr. Saginaw seated around the table. Ma and Pa looked thinner and paler than usual. And Mr. Saginaw hadn't even started fixing breakfast.

Something's wrong, Jonathan thought. But all he said was, "Good evening."

"Good evening," replied Ma and Pa and Mr. Saginaw.

Then Ma said, "'Jonathan, we have news for you."

Jonathan sank into his chair.

"It is time to move again," Ma went on.

"Really?" Jonathan replied. He had sort of liked the house they were living in.

"Yes," said Ma, "we will move tomorrow night. And now Pa and I must be on our way. We will have to get in a good night's work."

Jonathan didn't even bother to ask, as he occasionally did, "Where do you work?"

The vague answer was always the same: "At the blood bank."

"So pack up your things tonight," Pa told Jonathan. "Tomorrow night we move."

And now they were moving, whizzing through the countryside.

Next to Jonathan, Mr. Saginaw snored softly. He slept with his mouth open.

Pa sped along.

Ma leaned forward in her seat. She peered through the windshield. She checked the rearview mirror.

Jonathan daydreamed about Charlie Bucket's trip through the chocolate factory.

Suddenly Mrs. Primave sat bolt upright. She

looked in the mirror again. Then she turned around and looked out the back of the car, trying to see around the little U-Haul van that was attached to the car. "Vlad! Vlad!" she cried. "Slow down! You must slow down!"

"What is it this time, dear?" asked Pa. "A mosquito?"

"No, the police!"

That was when Jonathan heard sirens.

"How fast are you traveling?" asked Ma.

Pa checked the speedometer. "Ninety-two miles an hour," he said proudly.

Jonathan was surprised. He didn't think the old car could *go* that fast.

"*Slow down*," said Ma again, but it was too late. As Jonathan gazed out the window, a police car pulled up next to him. The siren was deafening.

"Wha—?" said Mr. Saginaw, waking up.

"Pa is going to be arrested!" exclaimed Jonathan.

The Primaves's car slowed to a stop. Pa pulled it to the side of the road. The policeman parked in front of it. Then he got out of his car and walked slowly back to the Primaves.

Pa rolled his window down. "Good evening, sir," he said politely.

"Evening," replied the officer, resting his arms on Pa's window and leaning inside, looking friendly.

"Any idea how fast you were traveling?" he asked Pa.

"Ninety-two, sir."

"What's the big rush?"

"Excuse me?"

"*Why* were you going ninety-two?"

"I am in a hurry. We must reach our new home by dawn."

"*Before* dawn," spoke up Ma.

The officer scratched his head. "Do you know what the speed limit is around here?" he asked.

Pa looked relieved. "Why, no, sir. I do not. I thought it might be about ninety, since we *are* out in the country and it *is* nighttime. So I apologize for those two extra miles an hour."

"You thought it might be ninety?!" exclaimed the

officer. "Look here, Mr. . . . Mr. . . ."

"Primave. Vladimir Primave."

"Mr. Primave, there is no ninety-mile-an-hour speed limit anywhere in the United States. Furthermore, the speed limit doesn't depend on what time of day it is."

"Forgive me," said Pa, "we did not see any signs."

"When you don't see signs and you're out on these county highways, it's fifty-five. Got that? Now may I see your license and registration, please?"

Jonathan glanced at Mr. Saginaw. License? Registration? What were they? Did Pa have them?

But Mr. Saginaw did not look at Jonathan. He was sitting tensely, staring at Pa and the police officer. Occasionally, he looked over his shoulder at the U-Haul behind them.

Pa removed his wallet from his pocket. He took some papers out and handed them to the officer.

"Mm-hmm, mm-hmm," the officer said as he looked at them. Then he handed them back to Pa. "Well, everything seems to be in order. Except there's a typo on your license. Says you were born in 1444. That'd make you, oh, five or six hundred years old. Someone must have hit the four key instead of the nine key when they were working on your license." The officer laughed, but Pa just smiled nervously. "All right now. I'm going to have to ticket you," the policeman went on. "Be right back."

The officer left the Primaves and returned to his car. He sat behind the steering wheel with the door open and the light on. He was writing something. It took forever.

"There are just three more hours until sunrise," said Ma quietly.

"I know," Pa answered. "Do not worry. We have time. We will reach our house before the sun comes up."

After a long while, the officer returned. When he was finished giving Pa the ticket, he said, "What's in the U-Haul?"

Ma and Pa both jumped.

"Nothing," said Ma.

"Our belongings," said Pa.

"Oh, yes, nothing but our belongings," Ma corrected herself. "That is what I meant to say."

"Mind if I take a look?" asked the officer.

Ma and Pa and Mr. Saginaw froze.

What was going on? Jonathan wondered.

At that moment, a call came over the officer's car radio. It must have been an important one because he forgot about the U-Haul. Instead he called, "Pay your fine, Mr. Primave. Have your license checked—and stick to fifty-five miles per hour!" He jumped into his car and roared off.

"How come the police get to speed?" asked Jonathan.

But no one answered him. They were too busy breathing sighs of relief.

"We will just make it," said Pa as he pulled back onto the road. "At fifty-five miles an hour, we will just reach our house before sunrise. Mr. Saginaw, perhaps you will help us with the trailer when we arrive?"

"Of course," he replied.

Jonathan drifted off to sleep and slept soundly as the night flew past him.

2

Tobi

Jonathan Primave couldn't sleep in his new house. He tossed around in his bed. He turned his pillow over. He kicked off his covers and looked at his clock. One-fifteen in the afternoon. Jonathan didn't know why he wasn't tired. The move the night before—the packing and the unpacking, and then the trip through the night—had taken a long time and had been quite tiresome.

"This is ridiculous," Jonathan said out loud. "I could at least read. Or—or maybe I could look out the window."

Jonathan had been told a number of times, by Ma and Pa as well as by Mr. Saginaw, not to go looking out windows in the middle of the day. But he couldn't help it. He was bored. And he was tired of rules he didn't understand.

Jonathan scrambled out of bed. He pulled the curtains back and let the shade roll up. Brilliant sunshine nearly blinded him.

Jonathan gasped. Outside his window were a greenish-brown lawn and several large trees. (Elms, Jonathan knew, from a boring tree book Mr. Saginaw had once gotten for him.) Beyond the trees were fields, as far as Jonathan could see, all the way to the horizon.

What grows in those fields? Jonathan wondered.

Also at the horizon were two tiny white buildings—one to the left and one to the right. Houses?

At that moment, Jonathan made up his mind. He was going to go outside, even though it was against the rules. He got dressed and tiptoed out of his room. He passed the door to his parents' room, which was closed, crept down a flight of stairs, and turned left into another hallway.

Very slowly and quietly, Jonathan unlocked the front door of his new house and stepped outside. He blinked and scrunched up his eyes. The sunshine seemed much brighter when he was actually standing in it than when he was just looking at it out his window.

"Ahhh," said Jonathan as he took in the summertime smells: tired, half-dried leaves and grass, flower-scented air, and parched earth.

He stepped down three brick stairs and onto a brick walk. He didn't remember ever seeing one of his houses from the outside, so he backed up and took a good look at this one.

It rose up three stories and was topped by a widow's walk. And it had a cupola on the left that made the house look lopsided. Several of the white shutters hung crookedly. Ivy crawled up the brick walls, but only in patches, leaving empty spaces here and there.

Jonathan wondered how long the house had stood empty before he and his parents and Mr. Saginaw moved in. Who, he worried, would paint the peeling shutters or repair the broken railings of the widow's walk or replace the missing bricks in the steps?

Jonathan decided to look around his yard. He returned to the brick path, walked down it, and reached a corner of the house.

"Aughh!" he cried.

"Aughh!" cried another voice.

Jonathan's heart pounded in his chest. He didn't know this person he had just run into—and he didn't want to wake his parents or Mr. Saginaw. So he grabbed the boy and clapped his hand over his mouth. "SHHH!" he hissed.

"Mmphh, mmphh." The boy struggled out of Jonathan's grasp.

"SHHH!" Jonathan hissed once more, just to be on the safe side.

The boy jerked away and faced Jonathan angrily, but he didn't make a sound.

"Who are you?" Jonathan whispered.

"I'm Tobi Maxwell," replied the boy warily. "Who are you? And why are you whispering?"

"I am Jonathan Primave. I live here. And I am whispering because I do not want to wake my parents or Mr. Saginaw. I am not supposed to be outside. I am breaking the rules."

Tobi frowned. "You talk funny," he said. Then he added, "Let's go to the summerhouse. We won't have to be so quiet there." He pointed across the back lawn to a square, open structure.

Tobi headed for it, and Jonathan followed him. When they reached the summerhouse, they climbed a short flight of steps and sat on a railing that ran around the building. From there, Jonathan could see the back of his house and, in other directions, miles and miles of fields.

"By the way," said Tobi, "in case you're wondering, I'm a girl."

Jonathan was startled. "Really?" Tobi was wearing jeans and a T-shirt, and her brown hair was cut

very short. "I thought girls wore dresses and had long hair," said Jonathan.

"Dresses? Are you kidding?" replied Tobi. "I thought it was just my hair that confused people. Where did *you* come from?"

Jonathan didn't know that Tobi was teasing him. He had no answer to her question. "From—from—" He had no idea where he'd come from, or where he was just then, for that matter. He hadn't thought to ask Ma and Pa. "We just moved in," he told Tobi.

"I know. Wow, *no* one ever thought *any*body would move into *this* old place. It's supposed to be haunted, you know."

"Oh. . . . No, I did not know," said Jonathan. "Do you live around here?"

"Sort of," replied Tobi. "When you're out in the country, no one lives nearby. Our house is across those fields, way over there. See?"

Jonathan nodded.

"We're two miles away," Tobi added.

"What are you doing out at this time of day?" Jonathan asked.

"Huh?" Tobi looked at her watch. "It's only one-thirty," she said. "I just ate lunch. I don't have to be home for hours. During the summer, or whenever school is out, Mom and Dad let me and my brothers do whatever we want, as long as we get our chores done."

"School?" repeated Jonathan. A funny little chill crept up his back. He felt like a child who was finding out that there really *isn't* a Santa Claus.

Tobi frowned again. "Yeah. School. You know— that place with all the desks and books and bad food."

Jonathan tried to hide his excitement. "Oh, of course. School. It is just that I have never been to one."

"Never been to school!" cried Tobi, amazed. "Wow. You are so lucky!"

"Well, perhaps," said Jonathan. "Listen, tell me something." Jonathan's mind was clicking away. "Do you really get to go out in the daytime?"

"Of course," said Tobi. "What'd you think?" Now she looked amazed. "Anyway, *you're* outside," she reminded him.

"Believe me, this is rare. My parents . . . my parents shelter me," Jonathan tried to explain. "Do you go outside often? Maybe even every day?"

"Sure. Geez, where *are* you from?"

Jonathan shook his head. "Do you mean are we from Pennsylvania or Arkansas?"

"Or Mars?" suggested Tobi.

Jonathan didn't get the joke. "Excuse me?"

"Never mind. *Do* you know where you're from?"

"No. Where are we now?"

"Hopewell, Maryland. The sticks."

Jonathan nodded. He didn't know what "the sticks" were, but slowly—very slowly—something was dawning on him. His parents and Mr. Saginaw had been lying to him!

"Tobi," he asked quickly, "do you have TV at your house?"

"Oh, sure. We're even getting cable soon. Maybe."

"And do you have something called a radio? And maybe a record player?"

"'Course. Well, not a record player, a stereo."

"And do you have a telephone?"

"Yes." Tobi was sounding impatient. "These aren't the olden days, you know."

"Forgive me," said Jonathan. "You see, *we* do not have any of those things. I," he went on, "have never believed they were real."

"You're weird," said Tobi flatly.

"I do not mean to be," replied Jonathan. "But tell me—where is your school? If there really is such a thing as school, I want to know what it is like."

"Oh," said Tobi. "Well, I can take you there. It's only about a mile away. Want to go?"

Jonathan looked at his sleepy house. Going to a school was surely against the rules, but he didn't care anymore. The rule-makers were liars, and he was mad at them. This was the first time Jonathan Primave had ever felt angry. "Yes," he told Tobi, "I do want to go. Right now."

3

Littleton Elementary School

Jonathan asked Tobi a lot of questions. But as Tobi led him through the fields to her school, she asked a lot of questions, too.

"How come you've never been outside before?" she wanted to know.

"Oh, I have been outside," Jonathan told her, "every time we move. But I just have not been out during the day."

"Didn't you ever look out your windows?" asked Tobi.

"Not during the day. We sleep all day. Besides, it is against the rules."

"Whose rules?"

"Ma's and Pa's. And Mr. Saginaw's."

"Who's Mr. Saginaw?"

"Our—our— I do not know what you would call him. He lives with us, and tutors me, and fixes my meals, and gets me books."

"Sort of a governess," said Tobi. "A man governess. I wonder if a man governess is called a governor."

Jonathan laughed. At last—a joke he understood!

"Mr. Saginaw taught me to read," he said.

"Oh," said Tobi, "is that how you know about TV and school and stuff?"

Jonathan nodded. "But my parents told me those things were made up."

"I wonder why," Tobi said thoughtfully. Then she added, "Do you believe everything they tell you? Do you follow all their rules?"

"I always have. . . ." Jonathan replied. "But . . . oh, well. Do most kids go to school?" he asked.

"Only all of them."

"My goodness! How about friends? Do you have friends? People in books always do."

"I've got lots of friends! Rusty and Eric and Sharrod."

"All boys. Are they your boyfriends?"

"*No way!* We're only nine. In fourth grade. You don't have boyfriends until you're much older."

"Oh."

"It's just that girls are dumb. I never bother with them."

"Oh," said Jonathan again. "By the way, why were you in our yard today? I am most glad you were there, but what were you doing?"

Tobi blushed. "My brothers," she said sheepishly, "dared me to go to your house after you moved in. They said— Well, this isn't very nice, but since it's not true, I guess I can tell you. They said that only, like, monsters would move into the old Drumthwacket place. And then you moved in in the middle of the night, which was kind of strange, so I decided to go look around for myself. And I did. And I met you. And you're . . . well, you're not a monster."

"Am I strange?" asked Jonathan.

"A little," Tobi admitted, "but I like you. You're okay. I like anyone who breaks rules sometimes. And you're breaking a big one right now, aren't you?"

"Definitely."

Jonathan and Tobi had been tramping along the edges of fields, following well-worn paths. They came to the corner of one field and found themselves facing a grove of trees.

Tobi marched straight into it, and Jonathan followed her. When they reached the other side, they came to a school playground. Jonathan had no idea what it was. He saw only silvery poles and long red boards and a roundish red thing.

"What *is* all this?" asked Jonathan.

"It's our playground, dummy," said Tobi. "Swings and seesaws and the merry-go-round. Oh, and over there are the monkey bars."

Jonathan nodded. "I have read about these things, but I have never seen them." He walked slowly toward the seesaws.

"Hey!" shouted Tobi. "Sorry I called you a dummy! I forgot you haven't seen any of this before. Want to go on the seesaws?"

" 'Go on' them?" repeated Jonathan. "I do not—"

"Here, I'll show you how," said Tobi.

Tobi ran to the seesaws, and Jonathan followed her. She lowered the end of one to the ground and told Jonathan to sit on it. Then she scrambled onto the raised end.

"You climb like a monkey!" said Jonathan.

"Thanks," said Tobi, "I know. Now, listen, I can show you how to swing, too, and how to climb on the jungle gym."

Tobi and Jonathan played for over an hour. "Goodness me," said Jonathan when they stopped to rest, "school certainly is fun."

"Ha," said Tobi, "this is hardly school. This is

recess. Real school is math and reading and work-books and teachers and sitting at your desk for hours."

"Where are the desks?" asked Jonathan.

"In the classrooms." Tobi pointed to the school building. "You want to see the room I'll be in when school starts?"

"Certainly," replied Jonathan.

"It's Miss Lecky's fourth grade," said Tobi as they walked across the playground. "Oh, here's the water fountain. Want a drink?"

Jonathan looked blank.

Tobi made a face, then showed him how to press the button and drink from the stream of water that shot up.

"My heavens!" exclaimed Jonathan.

"Hey, can I give you a tip?" asked Tobi. "Don't say 'My heavens' in front of any other kids. Or 'My goodness' or 'Goodness me.' Kids don't talk like that."

"All right," said Jonathan, wondering when he would ever see other kids.

Tobi took a drink, then peered through a window of the school building. "Okay," she said to Jonathan, "this is Littleton Elementary School, and *this*" (she rapped on the window) "is Miss Lecky's fourth-grade classroom."

Jonathan put his hands to the glass. He peered-inside and saw neat rows of desks and chairs, and one big desk.

"Who gets that big desk?" he asked.

"Miss Lecky, dum— I mean, it's the teacher's."

Jonathan continued to peer inside. "I see a science chart," he said, "and a lot of books. . . . I like books. School looks like fun, Tobi."

"We-ell . . . I guess it *can* be. Sometimes. Our class had a spelling bee with Mr. Proctor's class last year and we won a pizza party. That was fun. And seeing movies or videos is fun." Tobi saw Jonathan's blank look again, but she didn't feel like trying to explain what movies and videos were. "Hey," she went on, "do you know about gym?"

"Jim?" said Jonathan.

"You know. PE. Phys ed. Physical education."

"Oh! Physical education. Yes, I have heard of that."

"Well, gym is fun," said Tobi. "It's my favorite class. You get to play soccer and baseball and basketball and volleyball."

"I would like to try those games," Jonathan told Tobi. He looked thoughtful. "Tobi? Do you and the children—"

"Kids," Tobi corrected him.

"Do you and the kids spend the day together when you are in school?"

"Sure. From before eight-thirty until almost three o'clock."

"And school always happens during the day? Never at night?"

"Right."

"And do you eat lunch together?"

"Yup. In the cafeteria."

"I know you do not like everything about school, Tobi," said Jonathan, "but *I* would like to go to school. Right here. Right here at Littleton Elementary School."

"Well," said Tobi, "how old are you?"

"Nine. I turned nine in May."

"Then you'd be in fourth grade. Like me! Maybe you could even be in Miss Lecky's class. Miss Lecky is pretty cool. For a teacher. And for a girl."

"Miss Lecky is a *girl*?" said Jonathan incredulously.

"Well, no, she's a woman, a grown-up. I just meant she's cool for a—a female."

"Oh. I *would* like to go to school with you, Tobi. What do you have to do?"

"You mean to start school?"

"Yes."

"Register, I guess. And buy some pencils and a notebook. But no pens. Miss Lecky doesn't let fourth-graders write in pen. Ink is too hard to erase if you make a mistake."

"All right," said Jonathan. "Register. Notebook, pencils, no pen."

"You want to see the gym?" asked Tobi.

Jonathan looked at his watch. "I better not," he said. "I ought to go home. If I do not get some sleep today, I will be exhausted tonight. And I want to be alert. I *must* be alert, because I have decided to talk to my parents."

"You have?"

"Yes. I am going to ask Ma and Pa— No, I am going to *tell* Ma and Pa that when school starts, I will be going. When does it start?" he asked Tobi.

"In two weeks."

"And I will be there. I hope," added Jonathan.

"Great!" exclaimed Tobi. "I guess I better walk you home, huh?"

"Yes, please."

So Jonathan and Tobi tramped back to the old Drumthwacket place.

By the time Jonathan was home again and ready to go back to bed, he had come up with a long list of questions to ask Ma and Pa and Mr. Saginaw.

4

Ma and Pa Dracula

Jonathan's trip to school had been like a great middle-of-the-night adventure. He thought he would be exhausted, but he couldn't sleep at all. His room suddenly seemed so *bright*. He tossed and turned. He watched the numbers on his digital clock change . . . and change . . . and change.

At last Jonathan's clock read ten minutes before his alarm was set to go off. Surely he could get up now. Maybe his parents were already up. He could talk to them for ten extra minutes before they left for work.

Jonathan tiptoed into the hall. His parents' door was closed. Too bad. Jonathan must be the first one up. He tiptoed through the hall and down the stairs. Just as he reached the bottom, the door to the basement opened and out came his parents.

"Jonathan!" cried his mother. "You gave us a fright!"

"Excuse me," he replied, "you startled me, too."

Jonathan dashed back upstairs. Cautiously, he opened the door to his parents' bedroom. He peeped in. Their bed was neatly made. It hadn't been slept in!

Everything is getting stranger and stranger, thought Jonathan. But he would have to worry about his parents and the basement later. Right now he wanted to talk to Ma and Pa about school . . . and several other things.

Jonathan ran back downstairs and into the kitchen. Mr. Saginaw was just starting breakfast. Ma and Pa were standing by the back door.

"You are up early this evening," Pa said to Jonathan.

"I know," Jonathan replied. "Ma, Pa, I need to talk to you. It is very important. Could you eat breakfast with Mr. Saginaw and me? Just this once? You never eat with us. And you look like you could use some food."

Jonathan could not understand why his parents never ate breakfast. They always looked so thin in the evening. And pale. Almost, well, bloodless. And their eyes were so dull. Surely Mr. Saginaw's oatmeal would perk them up.

"I am sorry," answered Pa. "Your ma and I must go the blood bank."

"No," said Jonathan firmly, "not yet." He drew in a deep breath. "Look," he began, "today I could not sleep. So I got up. I went for a walk outside—"

"*Outside?*" asked Ma with a gasp. She sat down at the kitchen table. Pa followed her. So did Jonathan and Mr. Saginaw.

"Yes," answered Jonathan. Ma and Pa looked horrified, but Jonathan continued: "I met a girl named Tobi. She was very nice. And guess what? *Her* family sleeps at night. She goes out-of-doors during the daytime. She says TV and telephones and stereos are real."

"Oh, well," scoffed Pa, "just because she *says* so—"

"And then she took me to her school," Jonathan went on. "I saw it with my own eyes. Tobi and I rode on the swings and the seesaws. We looked through the windows of the school. We saw Miss Lecky's room. That is where Tobi will go to fourth grade. I saw the little desks and the big desk. Tobi said all chil—I mean, kids—go to school. Why do I not go? And why did you tell me school is not real?"

Jonathan glared at his parents and Mr. Saginaw. He waited for their answer.

Ma frowned. Pa glowered back at Jonathan. "You broke the rules," he reminded him sternly.

"You lied to me," Jonathan replied.

"Harrumph," said Mr. Saginaw.

Ma and Pa looked crossly at Mr. Saginaw. Everyone was tired of hearing him harrumph.

"I want to go to school," said Jonathan flatly.

Ma and Pa gasped. Ma patted the coil of hair on her head. She smoothed her filmy gown. At last she turned to Pa. "We knew this would happen one day," she said to him. "But I did not expect it this soon. He is still so young."

Pa nodded. "I suppose we will have to get used to the idea, though."

"Going to school would be a big change," Ma told Jonathan. "You would have to start sleeping during the night and getting up in the morning. You and Pa and I would hardly see each other."

"Why cannot you and Pa sleep at night, too?" asked Jonathan. "Tobi says that is what everyone does."

"We are not everyone," Pa informed him. "But we will let you go to school. I suppose," he continued wearily, "that Mr. Saginaw would no longer be your tutor."

Jonathan nodded.

"But he can help you with anything you need

during the day," Pa went on. "He will buy you a notebook and whatever you need for school. He will drive you to the library. He will be here to help you with, well, anything."

"But where will you be?" asked Jonathan nervously.

"Oh, we will be here, but we will be asleep," Pa spoke up. "As we told you, we will continue to sleep during the day and, um, work at night."

"You might have some trouble changing your sleeping habits," said Ma. "Learning to sleep when it is dark and going to school when it is light. However, if you start to switch now, you should be used to the new routine by the time school begins. We certainly will miss you, though."

"But why?" asked Jonathan. "Why can you and Pa not switch, too? I do not think anyone else sleeps during the day and stays up all night. Why do you have to?" Jonathan paused. He felt confused and angry. "Am I adopted?" he asked suddenly. "I am so different from you and Pa. We are not alike at all. I *am* adopted, am I not?"

Ma and Pa looked at each other for a long time. Their eyes were wide. At last Pa said, "All right, Jonathan, it is time you knew the truth."

So I *am* adopted, thought Jonathan. I just knew it.

"Your mother and I," Pa began, then he looked

helplessly at Ma. "Oh, I cannot tell him!" he cried. "You do it."

Ma sighed. "All right," she said, "here is the truth, Jonathan. Your father and I are vampires."

Jonathan laughed. "Ma!" he exclaimed. "Tell me the *real* truth. I can take it."

"That *is* the truth," said Mr. Saginaw slowly. "Remember that book on, er, monsters that I got for you at the library last week?"

"Yes," replied Jonathan.

"Go get it, please."

With a searching look at his parents, Jonathan got up. He found the book in his room. Then be brought it back downstairs.

"Turn to chapter seven," instructed Mr. Saginaw.

Jonathan did so. "It is called 'How to Recognize a Vampire,' " he said.

Mr. Saginaw nodded, meaning for Jonathan to begin reading.

"Well," said Jonathan, "it says, 'There are several signs to check for if you suspect that someone is a vampire. Vampires fear the sun.' " He looked nervously at Ma and Pa. Then he turned back to the book. " 'They cast no shadows.' "

Pa held his hand under a lamp. Jonathan looked at the table below. No shadow. He gulped, but kept on reading. " 'They are not reflected in mirrors.' "

"Which is precisely why we have no mirrors," said Ma. "They would be a waste of money."

"There are mirrors in the bathrooms of this house," Jonathan pointed out. "If you expect me to believe that you are vampires you will have to prove it."

"Very well," said Ma with a sigh.

She and Pa, Jonathan, and Mr. Saginaw walked into the bathroom next to the kitchen. The four of them stood in front of the mirror. Jonathan saw only himself and Mr. Saginaw.

"Upon my word!" he exclaimed. "So you are not a vampire?" he said to Mr. Saginaw as the four of them went back to their places at the table.

"No," replied his tutor. "Someone shall explain about that later."

After a wary glance at Ma and Pa, Jonathan returned to the book. He felt very much as if he had swallowed a rock. " 'Vampires have long clawlike nails,' " he read, " 'ice-cold skin, and fangs. Before eating, they are very thin, their skin is deathly white, and their eyes appear lifeless. After eating, they look much fatter—"

"Well, I should not say *fatter*," interrupted Ma.

"—their skin is flushed with blood, and their eyes are bright.' " Jonathan didn't have to check any of those signs. He had noticed them all. " 'Some people also believe that vampires are quite ugly,' " he read, " 'have hairy palms, pointed ears, eyebrows that meet over their noses, and extremely bad breath.' "

"Thank goodness we are not of *that* variety," said Ma with a shudder, looking at her smooth hands. "I would just *die* if that were so."

Ma laughed at her own joke. So did Pa and Mr. Saginaw.

But Jonathan couldn't. "All right," he said to Ma and Pa, "if you are vampires, then what am I? Where did I come from? And what is Mr. Saginaw?"

"You, my lovely boy," replied Ma fondly, "are our son. You are adopted."

"I thought so," muttered Jonathan.

"We wanted a child badly," Ma went on, "but we are centuries old. Our only hope was to adopt a child. And so we did."

"Lucky me," said Jonathan.

"And Mr. Saginaw is our, um, helper," put in Pa. "Like you, he is mortal. He is alive and human. And he does anything for us that must be done during daylight hours, catching sleep when he can. That is his job. Also to care for you."

Jonathan shook his head. "I do not believe this.

I just do not believe it."

"Think about our names," said Pa. "They tell part of the story. For instance, our last name is an anagram. Switch around the letters in 'Primave' and you get 'vampire.' And my first name," Pa went on proudly, "is Vladimir. I named myself for Vlad the Impaler, a horrible Romanian ruler of the fifteenth century. *His* father was Vlad the Devil. 'Devil' can be translated into the word 'Dracul.' "

"I," said Ma, "am Elizabeth, named for Elizabeth Bathory, a female vampire of long ago."

"I suppose I am named for some awful vampire, too," said Jonathan disgustedly.

"Certainly not," exclaimed Ma. "You were named for Jonathan Harker."

"Oh! I know him! He was the hero in *Dracula*!" cried Jonathan. "He was the good g— I mean, he was human."

Ma and Pa nodded, and Mr. Saginaw harrumphed and looked pleased.

"But," said Jonathan, frowning suddenly, "how did you become vampires? You were not born that way . . . were you?"

"No," said Pa. "We were bitten—for our blood— by other vampires. When we realized we could not change what had happened to us, we decided to accept ourselves as vampires, and to stay together.

We were already married. We took on our new names and, well, we adjusted to staying out of the sun and to living on blood."

Jonathan shuddered. "Where do you get your blood?" he couldn't help asking.

"At blood banks, mostly," replied Ma. "As we leave the house, we turn into bats—"

"Turn into bats?" cried Jonathan. "You turn into *bats*? I refuse to believe that my parents turn into bats every night."

"Jonathan," said Ma gently, "all vampires do that. If it upsets you, I am sorry. But that is what we do. Then we fly to the local blood bank, find some small opening to squeeze through, change back to our vampire forms, and have a nice meal." She sighed, looking quite satisfied.

"You mean you do not *work* at the blood bank?" asked Jonathan.

"No," Ma answered, "we do not need to work. We have plenty of money. Old money."

Jonathan nodded. "Do people not notice that you have been in their blood banks?" he wondered. "Do they not see that the supply is getting low?"

"Yes," said Pa sadly, "they do. Well, they do not know that vampires have been flying in, but they do see the supply dwindling. And they become suspicious. That is why we must move so often."

"What happens if you cannot get into the blood bank, or if there is not enough blood in it?"

Pa cleared his throat. "We have to take . . . other measures," he replied vaguely. "And if the supply is desperately low, then we must move."

"Do you ever kill humans?" Jonathan exclaimed with a gasp. He would have to remember never to let Tobi near his house again. At least at night.

But Ma answered, "Of course not! We are much more civilized than that."

Jonathan hoped so. But he wondered just what Ma and Pa would do if they were *very* hungry, or if they were lazy and didn't feel like going to the blood bank.

He tried to take everything in. His life was falling into place. He understood now why his family moved so often, why they always lived far out in the country, where his parents went at night, and why they looked so awful each evening before they left for the blood bank.

"I suppose," he said, "that you do not sleep in the bedroom. You must sleep in the basement. Vampires do."

"That is right," agreed Ma. "Our coffins are there. Mr. Saginaw used to open and close the door to our bedroom so that you would think we slept there."

"May I see the coffins?" asked Jonathan.

"I suppose so," answered Pa. He glanced at Ma. Ma shrugged.

Then Mr. and Mrs. Primave led the way to the basement. Ma turned on the light, and she and Pa went down the stairs. Jonathan and Mr. Saginaw followed them to the dimmest corner of the basement. There, side by side, were two coffins, one white, one brown. Jonathan had never seen them before. Ma and Pa and Mr. Saginaw must have kept them well-hidden during moves.

"The white one is mine," said Ma.

"We must have them with us at all times," added Pa.

"Were they in the U-Haul trailer when we were driving here?" Jonathan wanted to know.

"Yes," said Mr. Saginaw, "they were carefully covered up."

"How lucky that that policeman did not search the trailer," said Jonathan.

"Oh, *my*." Mr. Saginaw put his hands to his temples as if he had a horrible headache. "That would have been a tragedy. Think of the explaining we would have had to do."

"And probably in the sheriff's office or at a police station," agreed Ma, looking especially pale.

"May I see inside the coffins?" asked Jonathan.

"Well, all right," said Pa, "but do not . . . do not get too close at first."

Pa opened the lids of the coffins. Jonathan crept nearer to them. Was something going to jump out at him? He tiptoed closer and closer and—

"My heavens!" cried Jonathan. He backed away. "What on earth is that odor?"

"Earth," answered Ma.

The coffins were filled with dirt.

"It is from our native country," added Pa. "It is something we must have."

Ma nodded her head. "We apologize for the smell, but the soil is rather old now."

Jonathan made a face. "You *sleep* in it? How can you stand it?"

"Actually, we like it," replied Pa. "You would, too, if you were a vampire. But we know it smells because Mr. Saginaw prefers not to get too close to it."

"Foul stuff," muttered Mr. Saginaw.

Jonathan nodded gravely.

"Cheer up," said Ma, "have we not told you that you may go to school like other youngsters?"

"Forgive me," answered Jonathan, "but I am trying to—to absorb some unusual news. I have just learned that I am adopted and that my parents are vampires." He headed toward the stairs, feeling angry. "And furthermore, for nine years you kept me from things I might have enjoyed, like television."

Jonathan tried to calm down. "But thank you for letting me go to school," he said sincerely. "I simply cannot wait for math class!"

5

What Is a Cafeteria?

The day after Jonathan learned the startling news about his parents, he began trying to stay awake during the daylight hours. And he had a talk with Mr. Saginaw.

"I would like to register at school," he said. "Could we do it today or tomorrow, please?"

Mr. Saginaw was cooking something at the stove. He looked quite busy. "I do not—"

"Puh-*lease*?" begged Jonathan.

"Well, all right," Mr. Saginaw agreed. "I will arrange something. Wear your nice black suit. That will be appropriate for meeting the principal. Your other suits will be good for school."

So Mr. Saginaw set up a meeting. It went quite smoothly. Jonathan and his tutor sat in the office of

Mrs. Hancock, the principal, and Mr. Saginaw said, "It is rather a long story, but, well, Jonathan has been tutored at home since he was quite young. I believe you will find him well prepared. He is an excellent reader, probably reading at the high-school level."

"Hmm," said Mrs. Hancock, "in that case, perhaps we should put him in the fifth grade."

"Oh, no! Please!" exclaimed Jonathan. "I would much prefer to be with my peers. I have met Tobi Maxwell and I would like to be in Miss Lecky's class with her. . . . I mean, if that is possible."

Mrs. Hancock nodded and smiled. Then she gave Jonathan a test, which he completed quickly. The principal looked it over. "Flying colors!" she said. Jonathan wasn't sure what she meant, but he was delighted to be told that he could be a student in Miss Lecky's class.

After Jonathan's school registration, the days crawled by. Jonathan learned to sleep all night and to awaken around seven in the morning. And he saw Tobi many times. But waiting for school to start was *hard*. When the first day of school did arrive, Jonathan was a bundle of excitement. He put on his brown suit. Then he changed to his blue suit. Then he checked his briefcase. Mr. Saginaw had gone shopping for Jonathan's school things. He had bought a pair of very grown-up-looking shoes he called wing tips, and the briefcase.

The best part about the briefcase was that Mr. Saginaw had filled it with everything a student could possibly need. Neatly arranged inside were pencils (sharpened), a pencil sharpener, an eraser, a ruler, a compass, a protractor, scissors, notebook paper, extra dividers for Jonathan's three-ring notebook, reinforcers for the holes on the notebook paper, rubber bands, paper clips, index cards, a set of colored pencils (for making maps and graphs, Mr. Saginaw explained), glue, a small stapler, extra staples, a hole punch, and some masking tape.

Jonathan looked at himself in the bathroom mirror. Blue jacket, white shirt, blue bow tie. He needed something else, so he took two of his colored pencils from his briefcase and stuck them in his shirt pocket.

Very studious. Jonathan was ready.

He said good-bye to Mr. Saginaw. Then, briefcase in hand, he set off. He hoped he could remember the route to school that Tobi had shown him. And he did. He made only one wrong turn before he emerged from the woods to the playground. But then he nearly panicked. There were hundreds of students on the playground! Of course, he'd known there would be a lot of students at Littleton. He just hadn't expected this many, or to see them all together. He was thinking about turning around and going back home when he heard someone call, "Jon! Jo-on! JONATHAN!"

Oh, thank heavens! It was Tobi.

Jonathan ran to her. "Why did you call me 'Jon'?" he asked.

"Because 'Jonathan' sounds too, I don't know, too much like a grown-up's name. It's nerdy." Tobi paused. "Actually," she went on, "you look sort of—"

"What is wrong?" asked Jonathan.

"Well, it's the way you're dressed. And your— your—"

"My briefcase?"

"Um, yes." Tobi bit her lip. She looked as if she were trying not to smile.

"But what *about* my clothes and my briefcase?"

"Oh . . . nothing. Come on, let's go to Miss Lecky's room."

Tobi crossed the playground with Jonathan. Nearly every kid (well, every boy) they passed called out, "Hi, Tobes!" or "How was your summer?" or "How ya doin'?" Except for one kid who called out, "Who's the geek?"

In Miss Lecky's classroom it was the same thing.

Jonathan entered cautiously, pausing in the doorway to look around. The room looked pretty much the way it had when he and Tobi had peeked at it through the windows.

While he stood looking, the kids crowded around Tobi. Tobi laughed and grinned. For the first time in his life Jonathan Primave felt left out—until Tobi pulled him into the room and said, "This is Jon Primave. He moved here over the summer. He's my new friend. He's totally cool—"

"*He's* totally cool?" repeated one boy, grinning.

Another boy snickered. "It's only September, and we've already found the Nerd of the Year," he said.

"Hey, kid, who does the briefcase belong to? Your old man?" asked a third boy.

Jonathan looked helplessly at Tobi. What old man?

But Tobi was busy glaring at the kids.

"I do not know any old men," replied Jonathan. "Except for—" He had started to say "Except for Pa," since Pa was probably older than six or seven grandfathers put together. But he realized he shouldn't mention that. "I do not know any old men," he said again.

Since Tobi was glaring at everyone so hard, there was a moment of silence. But finally the first boy, whose name was Rusty Benoit, said to Jonathan,

"Nice shoes."

The rest of the kids looked at Jonathan's feet and began to laugh. Tobi put an end to it. "Shut up!" she cried. "This just shows how much you know. Jon happens to be an expert on monsters and ghosts. He's read millions of books about them. And he moved into the old Drumthwacket place," she added meaningfully.

Monsters? Ghosts? The Drumthwacket place? The kids looked at Jonathan with respect.

Then Tobi added, "Get this. He's never been to school before."

"No kidding," said another boy, whose name turned out to be Sharrod Peters. "He's never been to school before? Really? I'd never have been able to tell."

Tobi stuck her tongue out at Sharrod, but Rusty suddenly seemed friendlier.

"How come you've never been to school?" he asked.

Before Jonathan could answer, Miss Lecky stepped into the room. The kids looked at her for no more than a second, then they scattered for seats. Tobi pulled Jonathan to a desk in the back of the room and sat down next to him.

"It's always better to sit in back," she whispered.

Jonathan nodded, not sure why it was better, and

set his briefcase on the floor next to his desk.

The day began.

At first Jonathan felt overwhelmed and embarrassed. He didn't know the Pledge of Allegiance—didn't even know what it was. Then Miss Lecky reminded the students about lunches and lunch money. Jonathan realized that Mr. Saginaw had forgotten to give him either one.

"Don't worry," Tobi told him. "I'll loan you some money."

When the roll call and the Pledge of Allegiance and the announcements were over, Miss Lecky said, "Class, welcome to fourth grade."

"Thank you," replied Jonathan. Tobi elbowed him, and several kids laughed.

But Miss Lecky just smiled. "We have two new students this year—Jonathan Primave and Caddie Zajack. I hope you'll make them feel welcome. And please keep in mind that Jonathan has never attended school before. He has studied at home with a tutor, so some things will be new to him. He might appreciate a helping hand every now and then."

A helping hand? wondered Jonathan. What was that?

Miss Lecky asked Jonathan and Caddie to stand up.

They did, and the room was filled with murmurs.

Every head, even Caddie's, swiveled around to look at Jonathan. So he was grateful when Tobi called out, "Jonathan likes to be called Jon."

"Thank you, Tobi," said Miss Lecky, "but please remember to raise your hand. And now it's time for our reading period."

Reading period, Jonathan repeated to himself. He must try to remember all these new things.

The next three hours passed very quickly. Jonathan found the work quite easy, but there were some things he just didn't understand at all. One of them was raising his hand. When he worked with Mr. Saginaw, he didn't have to raise his hand. But Miss Lecky insisted on it. "No calling out, please," she kept saying.

"Why not?" Jonathan finally asked. He really needed to know.

Before Miss Lecky could answer him, Sharrod began waving his hand wildly. "Miss Lecky! Miss Lecky!"

"What is it, Sharrod?" she replied.

"Jonathan just called out. You said, 'No calling out, please,' and he called out. He said, 'Why not?' "

"Thank you, Sharrod—"

"Excuse me, Miss Lecky," Jonathan spoke up, "but did Sharrod not just call out himself? He was saying, 'Miss Lecky, Miss Lecky' while he was still waving his hand. Is that not calling out?"

"But, Miss Lecky, now *Jonathan* just called out," said Sharrod.

"So did you, Sharrod," spoke up Tobi.

"So did you, Tobi," said a friend of Tobi's named Eric Davis.

"So did you, Eric," said Sharrod.

Miss Lecky closed her eyes for a moment. When she opened them, she held up both hands. "Class!" she said loudly.

Everyone stopped talking.

"Jonathan," said Miss Lecky patiently, "we raise our hands so that *this* will not happen. When we call out, the room becomes noisy and we are distracted from our work. Do you understand?"

Jonathan raised his hand.

"Yes?" said Miss Lecky.

"I think so," Jonathan replied.

Miss Lecky closed her eyes again briefly. "Good," she said.

At last it was lunchtime.

"I love lunch—but I hate the cafeteria," said Tobi with a groan.

"What is a cafeteria?" asked Jonathan, as his class walked down the hall.

Rusty, Eric, and Sharrod snickered.

Jonathan had a feeling he should know what a cafeteria was. He'd read the word in books. He just couldn't remember what it meant.

"It's the place where you get your food, dum—Jon," Tobi whispered. "You stick with me. I have to loan you money, anyway."

Jonathan wasn't about to leave Tobi. How could he? Tobi knew everything about school; Jonathan knew nothing.

As Jonathan and his class walked down the hallway, Jonathan heard a noise that grew louder and louder. Then Miss Lecky opened a door and the noise became a roar.

"Well, this is it," said Tobi. "Littleton's good old cafeteria."

Jonathan stepped into one of the biggest rooms he'd ever seen. It was filled with long tables, and each table was filled with kids. And lunches.

"My heavens," said Jonathan.

Tobi nudged him. "Don't say that, remember?"

"What should I say?"

"Awesome."

"Awesome," murmured Jonathan.

"Now, come on, let's get our lunches before the line's too long. You've only got two choices at this school—hot lunch or bring your own."

"What is the hot lunch?" asked Jonathan.

"Um," said Tobi, straining to see, "pizzaburgers, salad, and Jell-O. Let's go."

Tobi showed Jonathan how to take a tray, a plate, a fork, a spoon, and a knife, and slide the tray along a counter. Behind the counter were three women. They were dressed in white. They were wearing plastic bags on their hands.

"Tobi," said Jonathan, "why are those—"

But Tobi wasn't paying attention. She had reached the first woman. She held her plate out. The woman dropped a helping of salad on it. Then Tobi slid her tray along. Jonathan followed her. He didn't stop in front of the salad lady.

"Young man," called the woman, "come back here!"

"Go get your salad," Tobi hissed to Jonathan.

"I do not like salad."

"It doesn't matter. They make you take it anyway."

Well, that was the silliest thing Jonathan had ever heard of. It was sillier than raising your hand. School, Jonathan realized, had rules. And he did not like all of them.

Jonathan went back for his salad. Then he caught up with Tobi in time to get his square of green Jell-O. He had never seen Jell-O before.

"Excuse me," said Jonathan to the Jell-O lady, "I

think something is wrong with this. It is moving."

Tobi rolled her eyes. "Forget it, Jon," she said. "Come on." She pulled him along to the last woman in white. The woman put two pizzaburgers on Tobi's plate.

Then Jonathan held out his plate. The woman put two pizzaburgers on it. Jonathan looked at them. He handed his plate back.

"Yes?" said the woman.

"May I have one more, please?"

"Two's the limit."

"But I will not be eating the green thing that moves or the salad—"

"Hey, quit holding up the line!" someone shouted.

"Yeah, get moving!"

"Jon," said Tobi, "come *on*. Your lunch is your lunch. Now let me buy it for you."

Goodness, thought Jonathan, school certainly was confusing.

After Tobi had paid for the lunches, she and Jonathan sat with a bunch of boys from their class. They talked about monsters. Jonathan knew more than any of them about vampires. He talked a lot. He ate his pizzaburgers. He did not let his fork touch the moving Jell-O.

When lunch was over, Tobi showed Jonathan

what to do with his tray. Later, she showed him where the boys' room was, how to work the copy machine, and how to hide gum under his desk. And as they left school together that afternoon, she politely suggested that perhaps Jonathan should stop wearing his suit and carrying the briefcase. Jonathan nodded wearily.

When Jonathan finally returned to his house that afternoon, he felt overwhelmed. But when Mr. Saginaw asked him how school had gone, Jonathan replied, "Awesome!"

He went to his room feeling angry, though. He was angry with Ma and Pa. Maybe school had been a little confusing, but it really had been awesome, too. And all those years since he was four or five he could have been going to one school or another. (He would have known about cafeterias and Jell-O.) But he hadn't gone. And why not? Because Ma and Pa had adopted a kid even though they were vampires. Then they'd tried to hide the truth from Jonathan. Why, he wondered, couldn't he have been adopted by a nice, regular family who didn't have to break into a blood bank every time they got hungry?

This is not fair, thought Jonathan, not fair at all. He sat on his bed. Then he went downstairs and looked at the basement door. Closed. Great. Ma and Pa were still asleep. How was Jonathan supposed to tell them about his first day at school?

He sighed. Oh, well. And then he remembered that he had . . . homework.

"My first homework!" said Jonathan as he ran back to his bedroom. "Oh, boy, time for math!"

6

Don't Bite!

Jonathan had been going to Littleton for several days when Tobi unexpectedly said to him, "So when are you going to ask me over to your house, Jon?"

It was lunchtime. Jonathan was seated in the noisy cafeteria. He was on a bench squished between Sharrod and Rusty. Tobi and Eric sat across from them.

"Excuse me?" said Jonathan.

"I said, when are you going to invite me over?"

Jonathan almost harrumphed, just like Mr. Saginaw. "Well," he said, "well . . . um, my parents don't let me have friends over."

"*Ever?*" exclaimed Tobi.

"Well, not for very long. I mean, they—"

R-R-R-I-I-I-N-N-N-G-G-G!

"Fire drill!" shrieked Tobi, and the kids ran out of the cafeteria.

Jonathan was saved—until the next day when Tobi said, "So are you going to invite me over? It would be so much fun. And I could just walk home with you and then walk to my own house. A cinch."

Jonathan didn't bother to ask what a cinch was. He thought for a moment. Then he said, "Sure you can come over. I'll just have to ask my moth— I mean, my mom what day is all right. Then I'll let you know."

Jonathan walked home from school slowly that day. What was he getting himself into? he wondered. But if he was going to be like other kids, he would have to invite friends over to his house, wouldn't he? There was one big problem, though. Jonathan wanted Tobi—or any friend—to find his house just like other houses.

Furthermore, Jonathan had read plenty of old books, and in those books, mothers were not only awake when their kids got home from school, but they were in the kitchen baking cookies, or they were gardening or working or setting the table for dinner.

Jonathan knew very well that if he asked Mr. Saginaw to put on an apron and be in the kitchen baking cookies one day, he would do it.

But that was not what Jonathan wanted.

Jonathan wanted his mother. He wanted her awake, reasonably well dressed, baking cookies, and not turning into a bat. Or biting necks. What if she suddenly became very hungry, but couldn't break into the blood bank because it was daytime? Jonathan tried not to think about it.

But did he dare ask Ma to be a real mother? *Could* she be one?

That night, Jonathan sat silently at the table in the kitchen. Mr. Saginaw was serving him dinner, and Ma and Pa were about to change into bats and visit the blood bank.

"Jonathan," said Ma, "you have been awfully quiet the past few days."

Jonathan ate a mouthful of rice, but he didn't say anything.

"Ever since school began," Pa added.

"School is not too difficult, is it?" asked Ma.

"Nope," said Jonathan without looking up.

"Sometimes," Ma went on, "you seem . . . angry."

"With us," said Pa.

Jonathan did look up then. "It's not easy being the son of vampires," he told them. "Especially when you're not a vampire yourself."

"We understand," said Pa.

"Is there anything we could do to make things easier?" asked Ma.

Jonathan thought hard. Should he ask Ma about baking cookies? She would have to get up during the day. She would have to see sunlight. . . .

Jonathan decided to take a chance. He put his fork down. Very solemnly he said to his parents (who were growing paler by the second), "I would like to invite Tobi to come over after school someday."

"Oh," said Ma, breathing a sigh of relief, "is that all?"

"No," said Jonathan. "When she comes over, I want you to be here like other mothers, Ma."

"Well, I will be here. I am always here during the day."

"Other mothers," said Jonathan, "are not sleeping in coffins during the day. Could you get up early— just this *once*—and bake cookies? And when Tobi and I come through the door, could you take the cookies out of the oven? *Please?*"

"Get up early? . . . Bake *cookies*? But, Jonathan, I have not baked in centuries. Furthermore, I do not need to bake," Mrs. Primave pointed out.

"I will be happy to do it," spoke up Mr. Saginaw.

"No," said Jonathan. "Thanks, but I want Ma. And I want her to put on regular clothes."

"Oh, Jonathan." Ma sank into one of the chairs. "Is this *very* important to you?"

"Very," Jonathan told her.

"Then I will do it. What would you like me to wear?"

Hmm, thought Jonathan, Miss Lecky always wears a skirt or a dress. Sometimes pants, but not very often. "A—a dress," he told Ma.

"All right, I have plenty of dresses. Of course, some of them are just a bit old."

"How old?" asked Jonathan.

Ma wrinkled her forehead. Then she turned to Pa. "Well, there is that one I wore when we went to the Vampire Ball. When was that, dear? Sixteen twenty-eight?"

"Or twenty-nine."

"So the ball gown," Ma told Jonathan, "would be, oh, three hundred fifty, four hundred years old. How is that?"

"Don't wear it," said Jonathan. Then he added politely, "Please, something more modern would be fine. Do you have anything more modern?"

"Most definitely," replied Ma. "Is that what you would like me to wear?"

Jonathan nodded.

Ma nodded.

It was settled.

*   *   *

One week later, Tobi walked home from school with Jonathan. While she talked about school and how dumb most of the girls were, Jonathan wondered just what his mother would be wearing when they got home. And would she have remembered to bake cookies? More important, would she have remembered to wake up? She had to get up five or six hours earlier than usual. Jonathan felt kind of bad about that, but surely she could do it just once.

When Jonathan and Tobi reached the Primaves's house, Tobi shivered. It was as run-down and spooky as ever.

"The old Drumthwacket place always gives me the creeps," said Tobi. "Especially on a gray day like this one."

"Really?" said Jonathan vaguely. His heart was pounding. He opened the front door.

He could smell something baking!

"Hi, Ma, I'm home!" he called, as if he did that every day.

"Gosh, your house is dark," commented Tobi as they walked through the first floor to the kitchen. "All the shades are drawn and—"

"Ma!" exclaimed Jonathan. "You baked cookies! And—and you're, um, all dressed up."

Mrs. Primave wasn't wearing her usual flowing,

filmy dress. She was wearing a different one. It was blue with sparkles on the top.

"Are you going to a ball?" asked Tobi, awed. "You're all— That dress is beautiful!"

"This old thing? It is just a housecoat. I have had it for years."

"I guess I should introduce you," said Jonathan nervously. "Ma, this is Tobi Maxwell. Tobi, this is my mother."

Tobi reached out to shake Ma's hand, but Jonathan cried, "Hey, Ma, I think your cookies are burning."

Ma turned around to check the oven, and Tobi whispered to Jonathan, "How come your mom's wearing sunglasses in the house?"

Before Jonathan could answer, Mrs. Primave said, "Why, the cookies are not burned at all. They are done perfectly." She pulled a sheet of gorgeous chocolate chip cookies out of the oven. Jonathan was certain Mr. Saginaw had baked them, but that was okay. So far, Ma was doing a great job. Well, a pretty good job. Jonathan couldn't ask for more.

When the cookies had cooled, Jonathan and Tobi put them on a plate and each ate several.

"Want some?" Tobi asked Mrs. Primave, passing her the plate.

"No, thank you, dear," Ma replied. "I am not a

bit hungry."

Thank goodness, thought Jonathan.

And then Tobi said, "You know what we should do this afternoon, Jon? I mean, if it's okay with you, Mrs. Primave." (Jonathan began to feel worried.) "We should go to the mall and play video games. Sharrod and some of the kids in our class are going to be there."

The mall? Video games? Jonathan had a vague idea what they were, but—

"Well, perhaps Mr. Saginaw could drive you over there," said Ma.

"Mr. Saginaw? Your governor?" asked Tobi.

No one answered her. Instead, Jonathan said, "Do you know the mall, Ma?"

"Why, certainly. I have flown over it—I mean, *driven* over there—dozens of times."

"Then could you take us?" Jonathan asked, suddenly feeling bold. He knew Mrs. Maxwell would take Tobi if she asked.

Ma looked narrowly at Jonathan. "But it is so bright outside today. And I have not driven the car in . . ."

Jonathan paused. What was he thinking of— asking his mother to go out in public. In the *daylight*? Imagine the things that could happen. Ma hadn't been awake during the day in centuries.

What if she got hungry? What if she turned into a bat? What if she forgot she was civilized and bit someone's neck?

And what would the sunlight do to her? Why did she have to stay out of it? Would it make her sick?

Tobi interrupted Jonathan's thoughts. "You haven't driven the car in . . . what?" she asked Mrs. Primave.

"In, um, in this area . . . much."

"Do you know the mall?" Tobi went on.

Mrs. Primave nodded.

Tobi looked confused. But all she said was, "Well, anyway, I can tell you how to get over there."

Now what? thought Jonathan. "You know," he said suddenly, "maybe we shouldn't go to the mall after all, Tobi."

"Why not?"

"Well . . . well . . . I don't think Sharrod likes me."

Tobi waved her hand as if that thought were the silliest in the world. "Who cares? And what does that have to do with whether you play video games? Don't you want to play, Jon? Big Video is where all the cool kids go."

All the cool kids? "Ma," said Jonathan, "Let's go!"

"But I said it is bright out today," hissed Ma.

"It's not bright, it's cloudy," Jonathan replied, which was perfect since Tobi wouldn't be able to see that Mrs. Primave did not cast a shadow.

"Who cares about the weather?" asked Tobi, and Jonathan just replied, "Ma is particular."

Ten minutes later, Ma, Jonathan, and Tobi were climbing into the Primaves's car. Ma was wearing a wide-brimmed hat with a veil, a long coat, and gloves—the old-fashioned kind that went up over her elbows.

"Are you *sure* you're not going to a ball or something?" Tobi asked. But Mrs. Primave had to concentrate on her driving, so she couldn't answer. She kept screeching around corners, jerking to a halt long before they reached stop signs, and slowing down whenever a car came toward her in the opposite direction.

Jonathan answered Tobi's question for Ma. "She has expensive taste," he said. It was the only excuse he could think of. He had probably read it in a book.

"Oh," said Tobi.

They screeched to a stop at an intersection. "Turn right," Tobi instructed Mrs. Primave, as she struggled to sit up straight, "where that sign says 'Straight ahead for the blood bank.' "

To the *blood bank*? Jonathan gulped. He glanced at Ma. Her mouth was open slightly so that her fangs showed. And her stomach was growling. Loudly. Jonathan was glad Tobi was sitting in the backseat.

Mrs. Primave sped through the intersection. Her stomach was growling and her eyes were blazing. She was not paying any attention.

"Right, right!" Tobi was shouting.

Jonathan leaned across the front seat to Ma. "Go back, turn right, and close your mouth," he whispered.

Ma obeyed. She seemed to return to normal.

When the car finally jerked to a halt in the Brownsboro Mall parking lot, Jonathan felt relieved.

"Big Video is this way, right nearby," Tobi said eagerly as they crossed the parking lot. "I hope you have lots of quarters, Jon."

Quarters? Jonathan looked at Ma. She nodded wearily.

"Goodness, I am hungry," Ma commented a few moments later.

"Well, there's a Cookie Heaven in the mall," said Tobi, "a Burger King, a little deli, and a Chinese restaurant."

But Ma wasn't paying attention. She had spotted something. Jonathan looked where she was looking and saw . . . the body of a dead squirrel.

Ma bent down.

"No!" hissed Jonathan. "Ma, you're in public!

You can't eat that. I mean, drink it." He looked at Tobi, who was frowning. "Ma—Ma can't stand the sight of dead animals. She thinks they should be buried somewhere," he explained.

"Oh," said Tobi knowingly, "then my mother is just like yours."

Not exactly, thought Jonathan.

The video arcade *was* nearby, and it was dark. Ma sighed with happiness when she spotted an empty chair in the darkest corner of the arcade. "I will sit down over there while you play your games," she said to Jonathan and Tobi, and she headed wearily toward the chair.

"You mean your mother's going to *stay* with us?" exclaimed Tobi in a loud whisper.

"I—I don't think she'll get in our way," replied Jonathan. He hoped Ma would go to sleep.

"But mothers *never* stay here. Ever. It's practically a rule."

"I can't help it," Jonathan replied. "She's tired. She got up early today."

"So I guess she's not going to go shopping or anything, is she?"

Jonathan shook his head.

"Well," said Tobi, looking at Mrs. Primave, "her clothes *are* . . . interesting. Kind of fashionable. I mean, they're bizarre and weird. Which is good.

Maybe the kids will think she's, like, a video queen."

Jonathan didn't have the vaguest idea what Tobi was talking about, but it didn't matter. He saw Sharrod and Eric and Rusty and a few other kids. Everyone was playing games, and no one teased Jonathan, not even Sharrod. So Jonathan and Tobi began to play, too. They laughed and shouted and won free games. Nobody gave Ma a second glance.

Nobody but Jonathan. He kept checking on her to make sure she was still in her chair. The moment she got up, Jonathan rushed over to her.

"Where are you going, Ma?" he asked nervously.

"Oh, just to the refreshment stand," she replied. She smiled at Jonathan. "Don't worry about me."

"Okay," Jonathan replied.

Ma was halfway out the door before Jonathan began to wonder about something. Did Ma eat or drink *any*thing besides blood? He didn't think so. Then where was she going? And had Tobi mentioned a refreshment stand? No.

"Tobi? Tobi?" said Jonathan urgently. He pulled on her shirtsleeve.

"Not now, Jon, I'm in the middle of a game." Tobi never took her eyes off the screen.

"I'll be right back!" Jonathan shouted at her. Then he dashed to the entrance of Big Video.

Where was Ma? He scanned the mall—and spotted a figure with a hat and gloves and a long coat. She was headed toward . . . a bloodmobile.

Jonathan ran through the crowd, darting between shoppers.

"Ma!" he exclaimed, catching up with her. He was just in time. Mrs. Primave was only a few yards from the bloodmobile. "Don't do it!"

Mrs. Primave turned around. "I am so hungry."

"I'm sorry," said Jonathan, "you'll have to eat tonight. How did you even know this was here?"

"I could smell it. I was sitting in that awful, noisy room just smelling it."

"How were you going to get inside? How were you going to get to the pints of blood?"

"I was going to turn into a bat."

"*Where?*" asked Jonathan, exasperated.

"In a phone booth," joked Mrs. Primave.

"Ma," said Jonathan, "it's time to go home."

"All right," she agreed with a sigh.

So Jonathan found Tobi, and rushed her and Ma out to the car just as darkness was falling.

One thing is sure, thought Jonathan, when you're the son of vampires, there is never a dull moment.

7

The Scariest Night of the Year

"No fair! No fair! No fair!" the kids in Jonathan's room were chanting.

Miss Lecky rubbed her hands across her eyes. She looked tired.

Tobi remembered to raise her hand for once.

"Yes, Tobi?" said Miss Lecky.

"Well, I just wanted to say," Tobi began, "that it really *isn't* fair about our Halloween party—"

"I agree, Tobi—"

"But," Tobi went on, "maybe we could do something about it. I mean, we don't have to take this lying down."

Jonathan looked around the classroom. Everyone was seated. He got prepared to lie down, but no one was moving. Hadn't Tobi just said, "We don't have to take this lying down"? Jonathan shook his head. Nearly every day, somebody said or did at least one thing he didn't understand.

Everyone in Jonathan's class was raising his or her hand. Miss Lecky called on someone else.

"We have never," said Marion Safire, "had no Halloween party. One year, the PTO couldn't hold it here at Littleton, but they gave it in the gym of the high school. We have never not had a Halloween party," she said again.

"It's especially not fair since we can't go trick-or-treating," added Rusty. "How can you go trick-or-treating in the country? There are miles and miles between our houses. Well, between some of them."

"I know," said Miss Lecky tiredly.

Jonathan frowned. He didn't understand why his classmates were so upset. Maybe this was because he'd never been to a Halloween party, or to any other kind of party, for that matter. All he knew was that every year on Halloween night, Littleton Elementary held a huge party for all the Littleton students. The money for the party was raised by something called the Peeteeyo. The kids would dress up in costumes and come to the gym where they could play games, eat candy, march in a parade, and win prizes for their costumes.

But this year, the Peeteeyo didn't have enough money for the party, so now there was nothing for the kids to do on Halloween night.

"I have the best costume of my life," said Caddie Zajack. "I worked on it all summer. Now there won't be any reason to wear it."

"Boys and girls!" Miss Lecky held her hands up. "Quiet down for a few minutes, please. I know you're upset. I understand that. I really do. So let's think about what Tobi said. Maybe we *could* do something about it."

"Raise enough money for a party for the whole school in just three weeks?" asked Tara Pushanski.

"No, I don't think that's possible," replied Miss Lecky. "But what about having a class party of our own?"

"In school?" said Rusty.

"During the day?" said Caddie.

"With cupcakes and room mothers?" said Sharrod.

"No way!" exclaimed Tobi.

Miss Lecky sighed.

"We want to do something at night," said Tobi. "Something really fun. Couldn't we have a class party at someone's house?"

"Mine's too small," said Tara.

"My parents wouldn't let me," said Sharrod.

"Mine probably would," said Tobi, "but I bet my brothers would ruin everything."

Timidly, Jonathan raised his hand.

"Yes?" said Miss Lecky.

"I—I think we could have the party at my house." This was the most daring thing Jonathan had ever said or done.

"Yeah! He's got a real Halloween house!" Tobi exclaimed.

"Right. . . . The old Drumthwacket place," said Rusty. "It *really* looks haunted."

"But it isn't . . . is it?" Caddie asked Jonathan.

"N-no," he replied.

"It's big enough, all right," added Tara.

"It's big and spooky and perfect," said Tobi excitedly. "Jon doesn't even have brothers or sisters who would bug us. I've been over there before."

Jonathan smiled nervously.

"Jon will have to check with his parents," Miss Lecky said. (Will I ever, thought Jonathan.) "And we *will* have to raise some money for the party. . . . Do you really think your parents will approve of this idea?" Miss Lecky asked Jonathan.

Jonathan paused as thoughts ran through his head. *He* certainly approved of the idea. A party at his house would help him fit in. It would be like going to school or playing video games at the mall.

He wanted Rusty and Eric and Sharrod to like him the way Tobi did, not just to sit next to him in the cafeteria because that was the only way they could sit with Tobi. Jonathan would give the best party ever.

Or would he? With Ma and Pa and Mr. Saginaw? On *Halloween*? Inviting twenty-three humans to his house was sort of like offering Ma and Pa a great big banquet. It was like saying, "Here are twenty-three necks for you to bite."

Of course, Ma had said that she and Pa were too civilized to bite humans. Had she meant it? They had never bitten Jonathan, and he was human. But biting a stranger was different from biting your son. With all those necks around, it would probably be hard to resist just one little bite.

"Jon?" Miss Lecky asked again.

"Well, um, well, I'll just have to check with my mother and father. I don't know," Jonathan finally replied.

"Tell them we'll pay for everything," Miss Lecky assured him. "Our class will think up some fund-raising projects."

"We could have a car wash!" said Tobi, without raising her hand.

"A bake sale," said Caddie.

"And," added Tara, "we could make copies of the

recipes for the stuff at the bake sale, and sell recipe books, too."

"That's a wonderful idea!" exclaimed Miss Lecky. Suddenly she sounded less tired. In fact, she looked almost excited.

"Maybe we could put on a play and charge money to see it, or have a carnival for the school, with a booth where you can dunk Mrs. Hancock in a tub of water, and a—"

"Tobi," Miss Lecky interrupted her, "that sounds a bit ambitious. We've only got three weeks. And we don't need a lot of money. Just enough for refreshments, decorations, and some prizes. And before we need any of *that*, we need Jon's parents' permission."

Jonathan gulped. Everyone was counting on him. Now he *had* to have the party at his house. If he didn't, the kids would be really mad at him. Maybe Miss Lecky would be mad at him, too.

Jonathan was pretty sure his parents would say yes to the party. After all, his mother had let him invite Tobi over, hadn't she? And she'd gone to the mall. But he'd have to make them *promise* not to get carried away if they were hungry.

That evening, Jonathan could barely wait for his parents to wake up. He had to talk to them before they left for the blood bank. Lately, they had been rushing off rather quickly.

Ma and Pa woke up just as Mr. Saginaw was putting dinner on the table.

"They're up!" Jonathan announced. "I hear their coffin lids!"

A few moments later, Ma and Pa appeared in the kitchen.

"Hello," said Ma.

"Well, we must be off," said Pa.

"Please," cried Jonathan, "before you leave, I *have* to talk to you! It's urgent."

"Could it wait, son?" asked Pa. "Your mother and I are hungry."

"*Quite* hungry," agreed Ma.

Jonathan cringed. He thought his parents looked paler than usual. And their eyes were dull. There wasn't a sign of life in them.

"It's really, really, really important," said Jonathan seriously.

"Well," said Pa, "if it is *that* important . . ."

"Three 'reallys,' " added Ma.

"And it won't take too long," Jonathan told them. "At least I don't think it will.

"All right," said Pa, "what is it?"

Ma and Pa sat down at the kitchen table. Actually, Jonathan thought, they didn't so much sit down as

sink down.

Mr. Saginaw served dinner to himself and Jonathan, while Jonathan tried to figure out just what to say to his parents.

Ma and Pa began to tap their feet and drum their fingers on the table.

"Jonathan," said Ma, "we really are hungry."

"I know," said Jonathan. And then, since he couldn't figure out how else to say it, he blurted out, "Ma, Pa, can I have a Halloween party here?"

"A party?" said Pa.

"At our house?" said Ma.

"On Hallo*ween*?" said Mr. Saginaw.

Jonathan nodded. He explained about the Peeteeyo party and how upset his classmates were. "I really want to have the party here," Jonathan added. "Our house looks spooky. And it's big enough for my whole class. Besides, I don't want to let my friends down, or Miss Lecky either."

"Oh, Jonathan," said Ma, and sighed.

"My class will pay for everything," Jonathan went on desperately, even though he knew that didn't really matter. "We're going to do things to raise money to buy food and decorations and prizes for games."

"I don't know," said Ma. "Jonathan, if you give a party, your father and I will have to be here. The other parents will expect that. We will have to stay at home, yet we must go out to eat."

"Couldn't you miss just *one* meal?" begged Jonathan. "No, wait. You wouldn't even have to miss a meal. Not really. Just wait until the party is over and *then* go to the blood bank. I don't think the party will last too long. I could even put a time limit on it. I could tell the kids that their parents have to pick them up by nine o'clock. How would that be? And afterward, you and Pa could go out. You'd have the rest of the night to eat."

"I suppose," replied Ma, "that we could find a fair amount of blood between nine o'clock and sunrise."

(Jonathan shivered.)

Pa shook his head. "What if one of the children wanders into the basement and finds our coffins?" he asked. "Then what? How do we explain that?"

"I'll put a 'Do not enter' sign on the basement door!" cried Jonathan. (He was beginning to feel hopeful.) "I'll tell the kids we're keeping our dog there while the party is going on."

"What dog?" asked Ma.

"Our *pet* dog," answered Jonathan. "They'll never know."

"What about our clothes?" asked Pa. "Or our fangs, or the way we start to look around mealtime?"

"Tobi didn't notice Ma's fangs," Jonathan pointed out.

"But Miss Lecky might."

"Then we'll tell everyone you have on vampire costumes for Halloween!" exclaimed Jonathan. "That would work! And you're leaving for a costume party at nine. That's why the parents have to pick my friends up then."

"Well," said Ma.

"Well," said Pa.

"Harrumph," said Mr. Saginaw.

"This is the easy stuff," Jonathan said. "Honest. What I'm worried about is, well, if you"—he nodded to Ma and Pa—"are going to be at home and hungry during the party, are . . . are my friends . . ."

"Safe?" supplied Ma.

"Yes."·

"I told you, we never bite humans. We've never bitten you or Mr. Saginaw, have we? Biting humans is quite impolite. At least in the United States."

"Do you *promise*?" said Jonathan.

"We promise," answered Ma and Pa.

"But what if you get really, really, really hungry?"

"Three 'reallys' again?" said Ma. "Hmm, I do not know."

"If they are *very* hungry, I can always shut them into their coffins," spoke up Mr. Saginaw. "I'll let them out later."

Pa nodded. "He has done it before. It is very helpful."

"May I have the party, then? Please?" asked Jonathan. He felt relieved. Sort of.

"Yes," replied Ma and Pa and Mr. Saginaw.

"All *right*!" cried Jonathan. He jumped out of his chair and leaped around the kitchen. He couldn't wait to tell his classmates the good news.

8

Silver and Garlic

The next Friday evening, Jonathan eagerly waited for his parents to get up. When he heard their coffin lids, he stood by the basement door so he could catch them on their way out.

"Guess what," he cried, as Ma and Pa opened the door, "everything is ready for tomorrow! Tobi says our committee will earn more money than any of the others. We're going to have a car wash."

Jonathan followed his parents into the kitchen. To his surprise, they did not get ready to go out. They slumped into chairs instead.

"What's wrong?" asked Jonathan nervously.

"We are . . . quite . . . hungry," said Ma faintly.

"But you're always hungry at this time of day," Jonathan replied. "Why don't you go to the blood bank?"

"The blood bank," Pa replied, "is getting, er, low."

"We have tried to be careful," said Ma. "A pint here, a pint there, hoping no one would notice."

"Did someone notice?" Jonathan asked, horrified. He remembered what Ma had said about having to move if anyone became suspicious of the Primaves.

"We are not sure," Pa answered, "but the blood bank *is* awfully low."

"Thanks to us, most likely," added Ma.

"So the past few nights we have been afraid to take even one pint," said Pa. "We were forced to kill a deer instead."

Jonathan, who had been sinking into his chair, jumped to his feet. "Kill a deer!" he cried. "You killed a deer? A poor, innocent *deer*? That's disgusting! That's *awful*!" He almost added, "I can't believe you're my parents," but he stopped himself in time. For one thing, they weren't his parents—not really. For another, it was too mean to say.

"Jonathan!" exclaimed Ma sharply. Ma rarely spoke sharply. When she did so, a spot of color flushed her pale cheeks.

Jonathan sat down.

"We never," said Pa firmly, "just choose an animal and kill it."

"That would be almost as uncivilized and impolite as killing a human," agreed Ma. "No, we search the roads for animals that have been hit by cars."

"Animals we can put out of their misery," Pa explained. "Last night, we came along just after an accident had happened. A driver had hit a deer, but afterward, he just started his car and kept on going. The deer was left lying by the side of the road. It was not conscious. And it would not have lived."

"We-ell," said Jonathan.

"So we had a meal," Ma went on, "but my goodness, we are tired. I suppose we shall have to fly around all of tonight, too, and who knows what we might find? Possibly just a rabbit. That barely makes a meal."

"Let us check out the blood bank," Pa suggested as he and Ma staggered to their feet. "Perhaps there were some donations today."

"I cannot wait until the annual blood drive is under way," said Ma, opening the back door. "When did those posters say it was to begin?"

"November third," Pa replied.

The back door slammed.

"November third," Jonathan repeated, burying his head in his hands.

"That does seem a long way off," agreed Mr. Saginaw. He had entered the kitchen and was stirring something in a pot on the stove. "However, your parents have survived these dry spells before."

"But don't you see?" said Jonathan miserably. "November third is *after* Halloween. After the *party*. If Ma and Pa are hungry now, think how hungry they'll be then."

The next morning, Tobi and her father picked up Jonathan, and then Rusty, Eric, and Sharrod, and drove them to the mall. Jonathan tried to think of some way to tell his friends that he would have to cancel the Halloween party. But they were so excited that he couldn't say a word. He didn't say anything about the party while they were washing cars, either. And at the end of the day, when Tobi counted up the money they'd earned and began leaping around the parking lot shouting, "We're rich! We're rich! Halloween party, here we come!" he really couldn't say anything. He didn't want to see Tobi unhappy. And he certainly didn't want to *make* her unhappy.

Jonathan decided that he would rather risk the party than disappoint his friends. So that night he went to Mr. Saginaw and said, "I need all those books on vampires and monsters again. Not the library books, the ones that are our own."

"Very well," replied Mr. Saginaw. "But why?"

Jonathan shrugged. "No reason."

Mr. Saginaw showed Jonathan where the books were, and Jonathan sat down on the floor in the den. He opened all the books to their tables of contents, and he looked in each one for a chapter titled something like, "How to Ward Off Vampires." He read and read and read. He made notes on a pad of yellow paper.

There were, he learned, two main ways to ward off vampires: with garlic and with silver crosses.

"Okay," Jonathan said to himself as he closed the books, "this is it. I will just have to be prepared for the night of the party. If there's any trouble, I'll get out some garlic or a silver cross. Of course, everyone will know about Ma and Pa if I do that—but at least nobody will get hurt."

During the next two weeks, while Miss Lecky's class raised more money and bought party supplies, Jonathan took care of other matters. Every time Mr. Saginaw drove to the grocery store at the mall, Jonathan begged to go with him. Secretly, he laid in a supply of garlic. He bought garlic powder, garlic salt, and garlic cloves.

And one day, he went to the jewelry department at a store called Bamberger's and bought a silver cross.

So Jonathan had his garlic and his cross. Miss

Lecky's class had their money. Halloween was just a few days away—and Ma and Pa were more tired and hungry than ever.

Jonathan hoped for the best.

9

The Cupboard Is Bare

"From ghoulies and ghosties, long-leggety beasties /
And things that go bump in the night. . . ."

It was Halloween and, Jonathan thought, it felt
like Halloween. A chill was in the air. Outside, the
last of the dry, brown leaves were falling from the
trees, leaving behind bare branches that scratched
the windows of the old house. Darkness fell early as
clouds scudded across the sky. Was a storm brew-
ing? Maybe. A stiff wind had blown up, and it
rattled the doors and whistled down the chimney.

"Spooky," Jonathan said to Mr. Saginaw.

"If there is a storm, it will certainly lend atmosphere to the party," Mr. Saginaw replied.

Jonathan thought that two vampires were enough
atmosphere for any party, but he didn't say so. He

and Mr. Saginaw were very busy. School had let out, and in just a few hours, the Halloween party would begin. There was decorating to be done, food to be set out, a DO NOT ENTER sign to be made, and one costume to get ready. Jonathan had decided to dress as a vampire. That way, maybe everyone would pay less attention to Ma and Pa—and be more likely to believe that they were in costumes too.

Miss Lecky had driven Jonathan home after school that day. In the back of her car had been two cases of soda; a carton of paper plates, cups, and napkins, and packages of plastic forks; bags of potato chips; some apples for apple bobbing; prizes for the costume judging; and more. Everything, in fact, that $150 had bought, except for the pizzas which Miss Lecky would pick up on her way to the party so that they would be warm.

"Look at all this stuff," said Jonathan to Mr. Saginaw after Miss Lecky had left.

"Well, we shall just have to get busy."

So they did.

The party was to start at six o'clock. By five-thirty, everything was ready except Jonathan.

"You better put your costume on," said Mr. Saginaw. "While you are doing that, I shall have to waken your parents. . . . Oh what a horrible job," he muttered.

"How do you waken them?" Jonathan whispered, wide-eyed.

"I go into the cellar and rap on their coffin lids. They absolutely detest it. But they must get up."

Jonathan nodded. Then he ran upstairs to put on his vampire costume. He had bought pointed teeth and was going to whiten his face with powder. Mr. Saginaw had made him a long black cape to wear with his black suit. His costume was very realistic. But as Jonathan was dressing, he grew more and more worried. His parents, he thought, were not only going to be hungry, but cranky as well from having gotten up early. What a combination!

When his costume was on, Jonathan went downstairs and made *certain* the DO NOT ENTER sign was hanging on the cellar door. Then he patted his chest to feel the cross that was hidden under the shirt of his costume. And last of all, he checked the jar that he had stashed in a cupboard in the kitchen. It held his garlic supply.

Jonathan was ready.

At six o'clock on the nose, two things happened: the doorbell rang, and Mr. Saginaw led Ma and Pa out of the basement. They looked terrible.

"Can you get the door, please?" Jonathan asked Mr. Saginaw. "I want to talk to Ma and Pa for a minute."

"Certainly."

Mr. Saginaw walked away, and Ma and Pa headed tiredly for the kitchen.

"How, um, how's the blood bank?" Jonathan asked, following them.

"Dry as a bone," said Ma crossly.

"The cupboard is bare," added Pa.

"When was the last time you ate?"

"Let me see. I believe it was Wednesday night," Pa replied. He didn't sound as grumpy as Ma did.

"We have been searching and searching," said Ma, "but we have not found any injured animals. Not even a mouse. And by the way, it was a mouse from which we ate on Wednesday. Just one mouse for the two of us. . . . But for pity's sake, do not worry so," she went on, seeing the horrified expression on Jonathan's face. "You have nothing to fear. We will be on our best behavior this evening. Dracula's honor."

"And might I say," added Pa, "that you are looking especially handsome tonight. That costume becomes you." Pa grinned, showing his fangs.

"Um, thanks," said Jonathan.

"Jon! Jon!"

Jonathan heard Tobi calling him from the other room. "I better go join the party," he said to his parents. "Are you coming?"

"Certainly," replied Ma and Pa.

Jonathan and his parents reached the living room just as the doorbell rang again. The next twenty minutes were very confusing. Kids kept arriving. Miss Lecky showed up, bringing the pizzas, which Mr. Saginaw helped her carry into the kitchen. And Tobi, who was dressed as an Indian brave, showed Jonathan how to work her tape deck. She'd brought it over, along with a stack of tapes. She said that any good party needs music.

Jonathan kept one eye on the party and one eye on his parents. Ma was playing her role well. She no longer seemed cross. "We are off to a costume party tonight," she said gaily to anyone who asked about her "costume."

"Hey, Jon!" Tobi cried at one point. "How come there's a 'Do not enter' sign on this door?"

"We got a dog," he lied, managing a grin, "but she's really shy. She doesn't like people at all. So she's staying in the basement during the party. Nobody should go down there."

"Oh, please, can't I just peek at her?" begged Tobi. "I *love* dogs."

Jonathan shook his head. "Sorry."

"Well, what kind of dog is she?"

"Umm . . . a collie. Okay, let's go."

"Where?"

"To check on the pizzas. How do you know when they're cooked?"

"Cooked!" exclaimed Tobi. "You don't *cook* pizzas! They come from the pizza place already cooked." She paused. "Oh, that's a joke, right?"

"Right. . . ." (If you don't cook pizzas, what are they doing in the oven? Jonathan wondered.)

Jonathan managed to get Tobi back to the living room where the party was in progress. All his classmates were there, along with Miss Lecky, Mr. Saginaw, and Ma and Pa. His friends looked as if they were having fun. Tobi's tapes were playing, there was plenty of food, and Miss Lecky was organizing games.

"How about bobbing for apples?" she suggested. "Come line up at the tub." (Mr. Saginaw had helped Jonathan fill a washtub with water. Now two dozen apples were floating in it.) "Anyone who can grab an apple between his teeth—no hands allowed—in less than sixty seconds wins a prize," Miss Lecky announced.

"Oh, how charming," commented Ma. "I haven't seen apple bobbing in nearly a century."

Pa elbowed Ma, and Ma fell silent.

A bunch of kids lined up at the washtub.

Ma and Pa edged closer to them. "Charming," Ma

murmured again.

And then Jonathan noticed something. When Sharrod knelt in front of the tub to bob for an apple, the back of his neck was completely exposed.

Ma and Pa moved even closer.

Jonathan glanced nervously at Mr. Saginaw, but Mr. Saginaw didn't look a bit concerned.

"Congratulations!" cried Miss Lecky, as Sharrod stood up, an apple between his teeth. "You're the first to win a prize!" She handed Sharrod a gruesome-looking windup spider and a towel so he could dry off.

Then Tara Pushanski knelt in front of the tub.

Ma and Pa moved closer. They were practically breathing down Tara's neck.

When Tara was finished, it was Tobi's turn. She got down on her knees, bent her head, and—

"Oh!" said Ma. She reached for Tobi's neck.

Jonathan's hand flew toward his silver cross. "Ma!" he cried. And he almost added, "Don't bite! Please!"

But Ma just said, "The tag on your costume is showing, Tobi," and tucked it underneath Tobi's shirt.

"Oh, thanks, Mrs. Primave," Tobi replied. And she put her face in the water.

Jonathan breathed a sigh of relief. His heart was

pounding, though. That had been too close. Much too close. How could he enjoy the party with Ma and Pa around? He couldn't, he decided.

"Ma, Pa," said Jonathan, and he pulled his parents into the kitchen. "Okay, time for a nap. Back to your coffins," he whispered. "All the parents have seen you. Miss Lecky knows you're here. You don't have to stick around anymore."

"You do not want us at the party?" asked Pa. He looked hurt.

"No, it's not that," Jonathan answered quickly, "it's just, well, you look so tired. Why stay up when you could be resting? I know how weak you are. Why don't you get some more sleep and then you'll have extra energy tonight when you're out hunting for . . . food."

"That is not a bad idea," said Ma, who looked as if she might not even be able to climb back into her coffin.

"Very well," said Pa. He took Ma by the arm and led her down the basement steps. Jonathan closed the door after them. His heart began beating normally again.

The party went on. After the apple bobbing, Miss Lecky and Mr. Saginaw served the pizzas. Then Miss Lecky gave out prizes for the best costumes at the party. When the prizes had been awarded, Tobi cried, "Let's play hide-and-seek! Jon's got the perfect house for it. It's so big and dark."

"Mr. Saginaw," said Miss Lecky questioningly, "is that all right with you?"

"I suppose so," he replied, "as long as everyone stays on the first floor."

So the game began. Jonathan had never played hide-and-seek, but he found that he liked it very much. He had been hiding and seeking for quite some time, when he noticed Mr. Saginaw harrumphing and tapping his watch. Jonathan looked at his own watch. Almost eight forty-five!

"Miss Lecky," Jonathan cried, "it's quarter to nine! My mom and dad have to leave soon."

"Right you are," she agreed. She stopped the game and gathered her students in the living room. Jonathan glanced around. Everyone was there . . . except Tobi.

"Tobi?" said Jonathan. He hurried into the kitchen. No Tobi. Maybe the bathroom, he thought. And that was when he saw the door to the basement. It was ajar.

No, thought Jonathan. Please, no.

Jonathan flicked a switch by the door. A dim light came on downstairs.

"Tobi?" he called again.

"Yeah?"

Oh, no, thought Jonathan. Oh, *no*! Had Tobi seen the coffins yet? At least she was alive.

Jonathan dashed down the stairs, his heart pounding.

"What are you doing down here?" he cried. Now that he'd seen that Tobi was all right, he wasn't quite so worried. He felt angry instead. "I told you not to come down here! I *told* you. I put a sign on the door and everything." Jonathan tried to catch his breath.

Tobi was next to the coffins. If she'd been any nearer, she would have been inside of one. But she didn't look as if she'd seen them. Jonathan tried to pull her toward the stairs.

"I just want to see the dog," said Tobi plaintively. "Where is she?"

"She's—she's— I think my father took her for a walk. Now come *on*."

Jonathan pulled at Tobi again, and as he did so, one of the coffin lids creaked open and a deathly white hand reached out slowly.

"Aughh!" screamed Tobi, as she saw it.

"Ma!" shouted Jonathan.

With a flourish, the coffin lid swung wide open. Ma sat bolt upright.

"Pew!" cried Tobi. "What a rotten smell!" And

then, "What's wrong with your mother? I'm getting out of here!"

She backed toward the stairway, her eyes wide with fright.

Behind Tobi, Jonathan yanked the cross from under his shirt and held it toward Ma. Immediately, Ma lay down. Jonathan hid the cross again. He didn't want Tobi to see it.

"What is going on?" Tobi whispered to Jonathan from the stairs. She felt her way backward up one step. Then she looked around frantically. "There is no dog, is there?" she said. "You just made that up so I wouldn't come down here." Tobi backed up one more step.

Jonathan had to stop her before she ran all the way upstairs and told Miss Lecky and the kids what she'd seen. He tried to laugh. Then he said, "Listen, Tobi, don't tell anyone about this, okay? These are just props for my parents' costumes at their party tonight. The—the coffins aren't as heavy as they look. But really, I don't want the kids to know how seriously my parents are taking this party. They'll think Ma and Pa are weird. And Sharrod and the others *finally* like me. So please don't tell.

"And of course we have a dog," Jonathan continued. "I told you—my father's out walking her." Jonathan turned toward Mrs. Primave's coffin. "Ma, you scared Tobi to death," he shouted.

"I am sorry, truly I am," came Ma's muffled voice from inside the coffin. "I just wanted to see how effective my costume is."

"It's—it's very effective," Tobi stammered.

Then she ran up the stairs, Jonathan at her heels.

Before reaching the top, though, Jonathan turned to glare at his mother's coffin. He half hoped it would open again so he could show Ma how mad he was. But the lid stayed firmly closed.

10

Moving Again

Jonathan's Halloween party was over. Miss Lecky and the kids had gone home. No one had been bitten. And no one except Tobi had seen anything strange or scary.

"Awesome party, Jon!" Tobi had exclaimed as she left, but she looked a little shaken. "Let me know when your dog isn't so shy," she added. "I really want to see her. As long as I don't have to go in the basement."

"Okay," replied Jonathan. He'd have to think up some explanation for giving away the collie, but he didn't need to do it just then. "Thanks for bringing your tapes and stuff. See you in school Monday," he called. He closed the front door and let out a huge sigh of relief. I did it! he thought.

Suddenly Ma and Pa appeared.

"Has everyone left?" asked Ma.

"Everyone," answered Jonathan. "Even Tobi," he added pointedly.

Ma didn't answer. She could barely stand up.

"Then we shall be off," Pa said weakly. "Wish us luck."

"No!" said Jonathan. "I want to talk to Ma. She almost grabbed Tobi."

"I could not help myself."

"We *must* be off," said Pa. "Jonathan, some things cannot wait."

"But—" said Jonathan.

"We are off," Pa replied, looking grim.

"Good luck," said Jonathan sulkily. "I hope you find . . . something."

As a precaution—in case they *didn't* find anything—Jonathan moved his garlic supply to the table next to his bed. He fell asleep that night wearing his cross. He wasn't going to take any chances.

Jonathan waited anxiously for the next few days to pass. November first . . . November second . . . November third . . . November fourth. The blood drive was under way. Jonathan was more relieved than he cared to admit. He couldn't stand the idea of

Ma and Pa stealing blood that sick people needed. It was horrible. On the other hand, they looked pretty sick themselves. They needed the blood, too.

On the evening of November fourth, Ma and Pa woke up early. They sat down at the table in the kitchen to spend some time with Jonathan and Mr. Saginaw before they left for the blood bank.

"Boy, do you look healthy," Jonathan couldn't help saying.

"Thank you kindly," replied Ma. "I certainly *feel* better."

"So do I," agreed Pa. "We had a real feast last night."

"Guess what happened in school today?" said Jonathan. "I got an A on a math test, I scored a goal playing soccer, and I was the first person Sharrod chose to be on his side in our spelling bee."

"Well, well," said Pa.

"Wonderful," said Ma.

"Oh, and this is from Miss Lecky and the kids in my class." Jonathan pulled a thank-you card out of his pocket. It was crumpled from having been sat on all day, but Ma and Pa didn't seem to care. "See? Everyone signed it," said Jonathan.

"Mm-hmmm," said Pa, "very nice."

Ma looked thoughtful. "You are happy now, Jonathan?" she said. "You are happy going to school, and being awake during the day and asleep at night?"

"Sure. Really happy," replied Jonathan, wondering why Ma was asking.

Ma nodded. "That is good," she said, but she glanced at Pa.

Jonathan had the feeling they wanted to talk to him about something.

Pa stood up. He folded his arms and began to pace back and forth across the kitchen floor. At last he said, "We had quite a scare when the blood bank ran dry. That was not a good sign."

"Sign of what?" Jonathan asked.

"Of how long we can stay here," Ma answered quietly. "We shall have to leave soon."

"Because people will be suspicious?" said Jonathan.

"Yes," replied Ma, "and because your father and I need a new source of food."

Jonathan nodded, remembering what had happened with Tobi in the basement. "How soon is soon?" he wanted to know.

"Immediately," replied Pa.

"*Immediately?*" cried Jonathan. "You mean tonight?"

"Tomorrow night," said Ma. "After we pack up."

"Wait a second," said Jonathan. "No! I'm not

moving. I have friends here. I go to school here. My life isn't just a house and books anymore. It's kids and playing outdoors and learning sports and eating in a cafeteria and raising my hand and Halloween parties. And—and it's Tobi and Sharrod and Rusty and Eric and Miss Lecky. You can't make me leave all that just because of your stupid blood bank. That's your problem, not mine." Jonathan turned away from his parents and Mr. Saginaw. He stalked out of the kitchen. He stomped up to his room. He slammed the door. He had never slammed his door before.

A few minutes later, someone knocked on it.

"Who is it?" called Jonathan sulkily.

"It is I, Pa."

"You can come in."

Pa entered Jonathan's room and sat on the bed.

"I thought you'd gone to the blood bank," said Jonathan. He looked down at his hands. He couldn't look at Pa.

"Your ma and I will go soon. This matter is more important. Jonathan, your mother and I did not realize how badly you wanted to stay here. We thought you would be happy going to any school."

Jonathan shrugged.

"What I want to tell you," said Pa, "is that we have decided to stay here. For your sake. At least

until the end of the school year."

Jonathan's head snapped up. "Really? Oh, thank you, Pa! Thank you, thank you, thank you! . . . Do you mean it?"

"Dracula's honor."

Jonathan grinned. He could stay!

Pa left the room. And as he left, Jonathan suddenly remembered his mother's hand creeping out of her coffin. He had to shake his head to get rid of the memory.

At school the next week, Jonathan learned to use a computer. He remembered to raise his hand every time he had something to say. He told Tobi that his parents had decided to give their collie to an elderly couple, to people who led a quiet life and whom the dog wouldn't feel so shy around.

And for the next few days, Ma and Pa seemed healthy. Then on Wednesday, they began to look a bit paler and seem a bit weaker.

"The blood bank is drying up quickly," said Pa.

"There was so much blood a few days ago," added Ma.

"Perhaps a hospital needed it," suggested Mr. Saginaw.

Jonathan opened his mouth. He almost said, "Maybe it's time to move again after all." Then he closed his mouth.

Two nights later Ma and Pa staggered out of the basement.

"We will be lucky to find a vole tonight," said Pa.

"What's a vole?" asked Jonathan.

"A mouse-sized creature," Ma answered shortly. She and Pa left the kitchen without saying another word. Jonathan ran to the window. He watched them turn into bats and fly into the night.

"Are they angry?" he asked Mr. Saginaw.

"No. They are hungry."

The night after that, Ma and Pa didn't even speak as they entered the kitchen. They couldn't. Ma leaned heavily on Pa's arm as he helped her out the back door. Jonathan ran to his room to check on his garlic. Then he put the cross around his neck. He decided to wear it at all times from then on. He sat down on his bed and thought. Ma and Pa had not said another word about moving, not since Jonathan had said he wouldn't move. But now they looked awfully sick, almost as bad as they had at Halloween. Jonathan sighed. What was the point of staying somewhere if his parents were going to be sick all the time? Anyway, he knew he wasn't being fair to them. They had tried awfully hard to help him fit in. And Jonathan could make friends anywhere. He could go to school anywhere. But who knew what would happen to Ma and Pa if they stayed in the old Drumthwacket house?

Jonathan knew what he had to do.

The next night, he waited for his parents to enter the kitchen. "Could you sit down?" he said.

"We must get food," Pa replied weakly. But he seemed to be having trouble walking, so he sank into a chair.

Ma sank into the one next to him.

"I don't know how to say this," Jonathan began, "but I guess I better say it fast. I—I think we should move after all. I can't stand to see you like this. You're so thin and pale. You hardly even talk anymore."

Jonathan picked up his spoon. He tapped it on his knife. He wasn't sure what to say next.

"Do you *want* to move?" asked Ma in a small voice.

"No," replied Jonathan, "but I think we have to."

Ma and Pa smiled at Jonathan.

"That is good news, son," said Pa.

And Ma added, "We love you."

Epilogue

The rattly old car sped through the night. Jonathan stared into darkness.

"Go to sleep, Jonathan," said Mr. Saginaw.

But Jonathan couldn't. No one else was asleep. Besides, he was too busy thinking. He thought how relieved he was that Ma and Pa had found a good meal the night before. They looked much healthier. He remembered saying good-bye to Miss Lecky and Tobi and his other friends that day. His class had given him a party in school. Jonathan had been the star of the afternoon, wearing new clothes that Tobi assured him were very cool. He thought about attending a new school when he and Ma and Pa and Mr. Saginaw reached their farmhouse in New Jersey. He was scared. He didn't want to start over again, but he had no choice. It might take awhile, but he would just have to look for another Tobi, another Sharrod, another Miss Lecky. He could do that . . . couldn't he?

He wasn't sure. He wasn't sure about any of those things. What if he *didn't* find a friend as good as Tobi or a teacher as nice as Miss Lecky?

Jonathan sighed and patted the pocket of his pants. He felt the wad of papers folded up in there. On the papers were the addresses of all the kids in Miss Lecky's class. Jonathan planned to write to somebody everyday. He hoped for lots of mail at his new house. Mail would be good, in case making new friends took awhile.

In the front seat, Mrs. Primave began to scream. "Vlad! Look out! Look out, Vlad! Look out, look out, look out!"

Mr. Primave hit the brakes.

EEEEEEEECH! The car skidded to a stop.

Mr. Primave turned to his wife. "What was it? What did you see?"

"I think it was a dead vole."

"Then you guys wait right here," said Jonathan. "I'll go get it. You could use a midnight snack."

When you're the son of vampires, thought Jonathan as he scrambled out of the car, you have to get used to these things.